MW00888329

MÉMOIRES

OF A

TRAVELHOLIC

MÉMOIRES
OF A
TRAVELHOLIC

Best Wishes,
Barb
Carole Kuhn

CAROLE J. KUHN, Ph. D.

authorHOUSE®

AuthorHouse™
1663 Liberty Drive
Bloomington, IN 47403
www.authorhouse.com
Phone: 1-800-839-8640

© 2013 by Carole J. Kuhn, Ph. D. All rights reserved.

Disclamer: The information-dates, names, places- that I have used in this book were that given to me by the various guides on my trips. This information was noted in my many diaries and should be regarded as correct for the time frame indicated.

No part of this book may be reproduced, stored in a retrieval system, or transmitted by any means without the written permission of the author.

Published by AuthorHouse   06/13/2013

ISBN: 978-1-4817-4144-6 (sc)
ISBN: 978-1-4817-4143-9 (hc)
ISBN: 978-1-4817-4152-1 (e)

Library of Congress Control Number: 2013909419

Any people depicted in stock imagery provided by Thinkstock are models, and such images are being used for illustrative purposes only.
Certain stock imagery © Thinkstock.

This book is printed on acid-free paper.

Because of the dynamic nature of the Internet, any web addresses or links contained in this book may have changed since publication and may no longer be valid. The views expressed in this work are solely those of the author and do not necessarily reflect the views of the publisher, and the publisher hereby disclaims any responsibility for them.

Table of Contents

Chapter One

1958 Brownell Tour

When I took my first trip to Europe, I had no idea that it would lead to 44+ more trips. I earned the money for it working at a pizza parlor after I finished my principal job of teaching high school English and French at Reily High School. My soon-to-be travel companion was one of my high school friends. It was convenient that she operated and managed two pizza parlors full-time so it was easy for me to get a part-time job.

We started planning the trip in 1957, and we both thought that it would be a great idea to travel before we settled down. Little did I know that I would really never settle down. For our European trip we chose Brownell Tours, and we would sail from New York to Plymouth, England, on the M.S. Italia, one of the main ships belonging to Home Lines. Home Lines was an Italian passenger shipping company that operated both ocean liners and cruise ships. The company was founded in 1946, and it ceased operations in 1988 when it merged with Holland America Line. Home Lines was one of the most highly regarded cruise lines in the world at that time.

Our voyage from New York sailed on June 7, 1958, and landed in Plymouth, England, on June 15. An 8-9 day trip by boat was very common in 1958. Our Brownell tour director was a nice lady, but I am not sure how much travel experience she had. Brownell Tours has been in business since 1887 and is still in business. "The World is Yours with Brownell Tours!" That was their slogan.

The *M.S. Italia* had lots of activities on board—concerts, movies, bingo, cards, table tennis, and dances, not to mention two sittings each for breakfast, lunch, and dinner. One special event interested me—a beauty contest on board. Prior to departure I had purchased a fantastic swimsuit. It was black nylon and rhinestone studded. It would be just perfect for a beauty contest.

Photo #1

Now here's the problem. How does one win the beauty contest but not get the crown? That's easy to explain. That happens when the judges are not familiar with the European Number System. The European seven has a cross bar on it, and if you're not paying attention and are unfamiliar with the differences between the U.S. seven and the European seven, you might read it as a nine. And that's exactly what happened. Well, I'll let the reader be the judge as to who really won the beauty contest. See Photo Number One. (Photo #1) I was #167, and I was told by the judges that I was the winner, but they inadvertently announced #169 the winner, not #167 because the judges confused the European seven and thought it was a nine. Well, after they crowned #169, they could not take it back. The Brownell Tour Director who had acted as one of the judges explained all of this to me, after the fact. Oh, well, this was just another bad experience to add to my list of things to forget in life.

Photo #2

Photo #3

Photo #4

When we landed in Plymouth and passed customs and immigration, we took a Boat Train to London where we spent 4 days. Then an overnight boat, the *Hook of Holland,* took us to Belgium where there were customs and immigration and a motor coach to The Hague. The remainder of our trip would be by coach: Brussels and the Atomim, (Photo #2) Cologne, Rudesheim, Baden-Baden, the Black Forest, Munich, Salzburg, Innsbruck, Venice, (Photo #3) San Marino, (Photo #4) Perugia, Sorrento, the Isle of Capri, with a visit to the Blue Grotto, Pompei, Naples, Rome, Florence, Genoa, Nice, Monaco, Grenoble, Berne, Geneva, Lucerne, Interlaken, Strasbourg, Nancy, Metz, and Paris. After 3-1/2 days in Paris we caught the Boat Train to Le Havre and back on the *M.S. Italia* for our return to the U.S. We arrived back home July 28, after first stopping in Halifax, Nova Scotia. One would think that a 10-day boat trip would be a welcome sight after such a whirlwind trip in Europe, but this was not the case. I welcomed the Halifax stopover because I was really seasick for the entire 10-day return trip home.

Photos #5

Photos #6

"A 52 day trip to Europe. What an experience!" My head was still spinning upon arriving in New York remembering all the sights that I had seen in Europe. I was fascinated by all the different cultures and all the different monies. That was a lot to cope with. In retrospect, I think the highlight of the trip was to the Isle of Capri and the Blue Grotto. That is very difficult to see today because the timing has to be just right. Also the weather plays an important part for the trip to take place. The seas cannot be too rough, and a sunny day is essential for the best view of the interior. After taking a large boat to Capri, you must transfer to a small rowboat-like vessel. When going thru the opening to the Blue Grotto, it's necessary to lie on your back until arriving inside the grotto. Then when you sit up, the blue of the Mediterranean is reflected on the ceiling of the grotto, thus giving it its name—Blue Grotto. (Photos #5 & #6) Since then I have returned to Italy several times, but the timing and the weather were never right to return to the Blue Grotto. Either the weather was not perfect, or the sea was too rough, or I didn't have enough time for the trip. It cannot be done in half a day. A full day is a must. Now that I got the Travel Bug, I would eventually take 44+ more trips to Europe, Asia, Africa, and around the world.

Chapter Two

1962 AAA and 1963 Study Abroad—Sorbonne

Photo #7

My Second Trip during the summer of 1962 was arranged by AAA. This time I was off to Portugal, Spain, and France. Since I was traveling by myself with my chosen itinerary, I decided to have a European courier meet me at all airports and train stations and accompany me to each hotel. I felt more comfortable doing this rather than stumbling around by myself. My flight was from New York to Lisbon. Then I transferred to the train station for a trip to Fatima to see this miracle city. On May 13, 1917, ten-year-old Lucia dos Santos and her cousins Jacinta and Francisco Marto, while herding sheep, saw a vision of the Virgin Mary who promised to share three secrets with them. Nearby was this well. (Photo #7)

Photo #8

The next day I transferred back to the train station for a visit to Lisbon and nearby Sintra and Estoril. Then I was off to Spain—this time by air. I flew from Lisbon to Seville, then Granada and the Alhambra (Photo #8), and Madrid. From Madrid, I took day trips to Toledo, then to Avila and Segovia.

Before leaving Spain I had to see Barcelona where I saw a series of 10 bullfights. If I were ever going to see a bullfight, this was the place to do it. However, I did not enjoy the fights at all. My sympathy was always with the bull. In the evening I got to see a Flamenco show which I enjoyed much more than the bullfights.

From Barcelona I flew to Lourdes, another miracle city where the Virgin Mary appeared to Bernadette Soubirous on 18 different occasions. The Grotto where the apparitions took place was dotted with crutches that the visiting lame no longer needed. From Lourdes I took a flight to Paris where I toured for 10 days. From Paris I found it easy to take day trips to nearby places of interest namely: Amiens, Fontainebleau, Malmaison, Versailles, Mont St. Michel, Lisieux, and Chantilly.

Then in 1963 I wanted to improve my French so I chose the Temple University Sorbonne Study Abroad Program. The Study Abroad Program housed the American students at the Foundation des Etats-Unis on Boulevard Jourdain in the south of Paris.

So from June 10,1963, until August 14, I had daily French classes in the morning, and the rest of the day I was free to explore Paris, and did I explore Paris! After class I took daily walks exploring as many Parisian nooks and crannies that I could find, but before my explorations began, I had my favorite lunch at my favorite restaurant—an Omelette Parmentier, which was an egg omelette stuffed with potatoes. The restaurant was right next to the Seine, so after lunch I would wander along the banks of a river that I had fallen in love with. The Seine is the lifeblood of Paris. It is unlike any other river that I have seen. Other rivers are commercial highways with barges and boats moving commerce, and their bridges are used just to get from one side to the other. The Seine has bridges unique to its own history and personality. Along the shores of the Seine is the history of Paris with its museums, parks, buildings, and churches all with their own tales. It is the heart of Paris and belongs to the people. The people, in turn, sit along its banks, stroll across its bridges, and peruse the bouquinistes which line the banks

Browsing the bouquinistes you can find old books, post cards, prints, and scenes of Paris. The bouquinistes are individual locked "boxes" along the sidewalks, and they contain the wares of the booksellers. If the bookseller doesn't want to open the box, he may opt to stay home, and his individual "shop" remains closed for the day. How nice to open and close shops whenever you feel like it and not have scheduled hours.

Although I had visited Paris on two previous trips, it seemed that I could not see enough. Even today after more than 25 trips to Paris, I still feel that there is more than 40% of the city that I do not know, but my love affaire with this city was only just beginning. When I returned home in the U.S., I would change my teaching direction from English to French. At the end of my Study Abroad Program, our group traveled to Dijon, Geneva, Chamonix, Grenoble, Cannes, Nice, Monte Carlo, Nîmes, Arles, Avignon, and Carcassonne, (Photo #9)

Photo #9

Carcassonne has a unique history about its name. According to the legend, in the 8th century Charlemagne and his Franks besieged the fortified city of Carcassonne for about 6 years. The city was actually starving to death when Mme Carcas came up with an idea. Take the last pig in the city, feed it well, and throw it over the walls to indicate to the Franks that the city was not starving to death but instead had an ample supply of corn to feed its swine. That done, the Franks analyzed the situation and decided to leave the city, and Madame Carcas rang the bell to indicate to everyone that the enemy had left. Mme Carcas rang (sonne) the bell to announce their departure. Hence: Mme Carcassonne. It's a nice story, but not too believable. There is, however, a stone portrait of Mme Carcas at the main gate of Carcassonne.

In Carcassonne I fell in love with the Fabrice Tapestries, which hugged the walls of my hotel, the Hôtel de la Cité.

When I returned home, I would order one of these beautiful tapestries. I wrote to Fabrice, the artist, that I wanted a tapestry with French Poodles. I gave him *carte blanche* to choose the design and the colors. That beautiful tapestry became the centerpiece of my furniture design, and it hangs today in my Great Room.

Chapter Three

1964 Study Abroad —Holy Land

Photo #10

In the summer of 1964 I took another Study Abroad Trip, this time to the Holy Land. As it turned out, this was a really good time to see this area of the world. All the problems that later would develop between the Arabs and Jews had not yet halted travel to those countries. There were no suicide bombers blowing up planes and buildings. Later on my trip around the world, we would not be allowed to visit many of the countries that I would see in 1964. Our trip began in Naples and the beautiful Amalfi Drive, (Photo #10) then on to Rome with all its famous sites. We also drove to Castel Gandolfo and a visit with Pope Paul VI, then a beautiful trip to Villa d'Este.

From Italy we flew to Egypt where we visited the ancient capital, Memphis, about 15 miles south of Cairo on the Nile. I couldn't pass up the opportunity of getting my picture taken on a camel when the opportunity presented itself. (Photo #11) Then we visited the Step Pyramid of Djoser at Saqqara. Egypt is certainly not short of pyramids. Next we visited the Valley of the Kings, the Valley of the Queens, and the beautiful Temple of Luxor with the Sitting Statue of Ramesses II. We visited the Sphinx on the west bank of the Nile for a photo opt. (Photo #12) Our last night in Cairo was spent boating on the Nile aboard a beautiful *felucca*.

Photo #11

Photo #12

From Egypt we flew to Beirut where the famous Cedars of Lebanon are growing, then north to Tripoli, the second largest city in Lebanon. Before leaving this country, we visited the Temple of Jupiter in Baalbek, the ruins of a beautiful Roman masterpiece.

From Lebanon we entered Syria and its capital Damascus. We saw the Street Called Straight that St. Paul had mentioned in the New Testament, in addition to St. Paul's Window. At the end of the street, we saw the house of Ananius, a saint who healed St. Paul's eyes.

Photo #13

From Syria, we journeyed to Jordan where we saw the Temple of Artemis at Jerash with its 11 Corinthian columns still standing. We stayed at the Al Urdon Hotel in Amman. We toured the Judean Hills where we had good views of the Qumran Caves where a Bedouin boy had found the Dead Sea Scrolls in 1947. (Photo #13) We had a good view of the Dead Sea with Mt. Nebo in the distance, a site where Moses viewed the Promised Land. Also in Jordan, we visited the city of Jericho where we saw the ruins of Elijah's Fountain. There was a good view of the Mt. of Temptation in the distance. Before leaving, we could see what was left of the walls of

Jericho. We got to put our feet in the River Jordan. Then we passed the Inn of the Good Samaritan before we journeyed to our next destination, Jerusalem.

Photo #14

Our visit to Israel included a stop at St. Stephen's Gate or sometimes called the Lions' Gate where Christ began his long walk to Calvary. Then we viewed the Church of Sainte Anne, the Pool of Bethesda (sometimes associated with healing powers), the Ecce Homo Arch, and the Dome of the Rock, Via Dolorosa, the Palace of Pilate, the Jewish Wailing Wall and the Church of Agony in the Garden of Gethsemane. (Photo #14) After the Garden we visited the city of Bethlehem. En route, we saw the Tomb of Rachel, a Jewish sacred site, believed to be where the mother of Jacob is buried. In Bethlehem we saw Shepherds' Field, and the Church of the Nativity, plus the Needle Eye Gate, a gate in several Holy Land cities that was smaller than the other gates, thus making it more difficult for men on camels to pass through. This Gate also is referenced in the Bible as the "eye of the needle".

Returning to Jerusalem via Kidron Valley, we visited the Mt. of Olives, a Jewish burial site and possible site of the Ascension. Then in Bethany we passed the Home of Mary, Martha, and Lazarus plus the Tomb of Lazarus. We also visited a site, which shows part of a wall supposedly a remnant of Solomon's Temple. Then we toured the Garden of Gethsemane, at the foot of the Mount of Olives, where Christ and his disciples prayed the night before the crucifixion. We also saw the tomb of the Virgin Mary, which is also at the foot of the Mount of Olives. In Jerusalem we saw a hill, the possible site of Calvary, also a cave-like structure, which is considered the possible garden tomb. There is a beautiful Palestine Archaeological Museum with an equally beautiful cloister, which today has been named the Rockefeller Museum.

One of the many highlights of this trip was a visit to the Hadassah Medical Center with Marc Chagall's magnificent stained glass windows depicting the twelve tribes of Israel. The windows were installed February, 1962. Afterwards we visited the Church of the Nativity of John the Baptist. Then later, we visited the Church of the Dormition, which was built on the site where the Virgin Mary fell into an eternal sleep.

Leaving the major cities, we followed the coast, visiting the port at Acre with its Turkish fortifications. Then we continued to Haifa where we saw the Bahai Temple, which seems to house a kind of generic religion. Not far from Haifa, we came across the ruins of Solomon's Stables at Megiddo. We passed several groups of Arab goats along the road on our way to Mt. Tabor, the site of the Transfiguration. We stropped at the beautiful Sea of Galilee in the Jordan Valley with a view of the Syrian Mountains in the distance.

There was still a lot more to see in the Holy Land. After the Sea of Galilee, we saw the Franciscan Monastery on the Mt. of the Beatitudes near Capernaum, home of the apostles. The rest of the time in the Holy Land was spent in Caesarea, Jaffa, and Tel Aviv.

From Israel we journeyed to Turkey with a visit to the Blue Mosque, the Bosporus, Ismir, the Gulf of Smyrna, and the House of the Virgin Mary at Ephesus. According to tradition, Mary was brought to Ephesus where she spent the rest of her life. Then we toured the summer resort town of Kusadasi on Turkey's Aegean Coast.

From Turkey we traveled to Athens, Greece, where we visited the Acropolis and the Parthenon as well as Hadrian's Arch and the Temple of Jupiter, on the Capitoline Hill. Later on we would visit Daphne and the Ismus of Corinth where the Aegean and the Ionian Seas meet. Our next stop in Greece would be Mycenae, a military citadel and one of the major centers of Greek civilization. A major attraction in Mycenae is the Lion Gate although we know little or nothing about its history.

Our next visit was to a 4th century amphitheater at Epidaurus followed by a visit to the famous Megaron of the palace of Tiryns, a 14th century monastery church at Mystras. We then continued to Olympia where the first Olympic Games were held. In the distance we could see Sparta. As we traveled to our final visit in Greece, Delphi, we could see Mt. Parnassus, home of the gods, in the distance. At Delphi we saw the Temple of Apollo. Then our final visit in mainland Greece was to a very impressive Byzantine monastery at Ossios.

At this point in our trip we took an Aegean Cruise to see the beautiful Greek islands. Our first stop was Rhodes where we debarked and visited the acropolis in the village of Lindos. The movie, *The Guns of Navaronne*, was filmed at Lindos. While there, we toured the Palace of the Grand Master.

Our next stop on our island tour was Crete where we saw the Palace of Knossos, the monumental symbol of Minoan civilization and the fort of Heraklion, Crete. From Crete our ship stopped at the beautiful Santorini, the island of volcanic eruptions, then the sacred and deserted Island of Delos with the Terrace of Lions. (Photo #15) Our last stop was the island of Mykonos. (Photo #16)

Carole J. Kuhn, Ph. D.

Photo #15

Photo #16

Chapter Four

1965 University of Utah Study Tour

My next trip in 1965 was again with Study Abroad in conjunction with the University of Utah. This tour included Norway, Denmark, Sweden, Finland, the U.S.S.R, Austria, Italy, West Germany, France, and England. The tour was designed to study music and art in Western Europe and the Soviet Union. We began June 26 in New York and ended August 15. In Norway we first visited the city of Bergen. Then we toured Edward Grieg's home in Troldhaugen. Then we were off to Oslo where we saw the Kon-Tiki Museum, and Vigeland Park with its many unique statues.

Next we journeyed to Copenhagen, Denmark, where we visited the famous Tivoli Gardens and the photogenic Mermaid who sits at the entrance to the harbor. We also visited Frederiksborg Palace in Hillerød. It was built as a royal residence for King Christian IV. In Helsinger we visited the castle of Kronborg immortalized as *Elsinore* in William Shakespeare's play *Hamlet*.

Next was a visit to Drotthingholm Gardens and Palace in Stockholm, Sweden. The palace is the private residence of the Swedish royal family.

Photo #17

In Skansen Park we saw some Swedish folk dancing. Next we visited a park established by Carl and Olga Milles on the island of Lidingö called Millesgarden. (Photo #17) Then in Finland, we first saw the Lutheran Cathedral, Suomenlinna, which dominates the bay. Nearby is the inhabited sea fortress built on six islands. It is a world heritage site belonging to Finland.

After the Scandinavian countries, we continued to the U.S.S.R.

Our first city was Leningrad, now called St. Petersburg. There we visited Peter and Paul Cathedral, the Winter Palace, St. Isaac's Cathedral, and the ship *Aurora*. Then we were off to Petershoff built in 1721 by Peter the Great. Today it's a beautiful yellow palace surrounded by fountains and gardens and is the Russian answer to Versailles. At the entrance was a black and white picture showing the palace as the Nazis left it during World War II. The Russians used all their ability and expertise in order to return it to its original state, and they shared no expense in this process made possible during a dictatorship. In fact, this beautification process was carried out throughout the city of Leningrad. The Nazis destroyed what they could during the 900-day siege of shelling and bombing, but the pride that the Russians have in their history would not let their destruction stand.

Next on our tour was Moscow. We saw all the usual tourist spots—Red Square, St. Basil's, Pushkin Square, the Space Monument, the Kremlin, and Cathedral Square. From Moscow we flew to Kiev and visited the Palace of the Young Pioneers, St. Sophia, and the Lenin Garden. From Kiev we flew to Vienna, situated on the Danube River. We visited Belvedere Palace and Schönbrunn Palace. From Vienna we went to Berlin where we saw the Brandenburg Gate, the Berlin Wall, and an East Berlin Cemetery. We could see Checkpoint Charlie where one could pass between East and West Germany with the right documents. This is a photo of the Wall and East Berlin Cemetery. (Photo #18)

Photo #18

The thing I remember best about this trip was the Aeroflot Airline trip from Kiev to Vienna. I had never been on an Aeroflot plane before. I was familiar with planes starting their engines and taxing to the end of the runway before taking off. I was not familiar with being *pulled* to the end of the runway, and then taking off as the Russian airlines did without the usual warm-up procedure. That situation was really scary.

Chapter Five

1966 French Language Study Tour in Reims

In 1966 I decided on a Foreign Language Study Trip to Reims, France, where I would have classes for 4 weeks at the University of Reims. But before the university study began, we would visit Paris. My trip would begin in my favorite cemetery in the world—Père La Chaise. Therein lies the tomb of the set of star-crossed lovers, Abélard and Héloïse, not to mention Edith Piaf, Chopin, Balzac, and Oscar Wilde. The list of famous people goes on forever. From there we visited La Sainte Chapelle, then headed out for a tour of France including the châteaux of Blois, Chambord, Tours, Azay-le-Rideau, Chinon, and Chenonceaux. Then we crossed into Belgium with a stop in the capital, Brussels, just enough time to see the famous statue of its little boy doing his thing, called the *Manneken Pis*. (Photo #19) Also in Belgium we visited the site of the famous Battle of Waterloo and Bastogne in the Ardennes Forest, where the siege of Bastogne took place. (Photo #20)

Photo #19

Photo #20

Then we crossed into Luxembourg where there is a large American cemetery containing more than 5,000 of our American dead, many of whom lost their lives in the Battle of the Bulge and in the advance to the Rhine River.

When we got to Reims, we checked into our living facilities, the Cité Universitaire. As usual we had morning classes; then in the afternoon we had arranged visits to area attractions. The main attraction in Reims, of course, is the cathedral where many French kings were crowned. This is the cathedral that Joan of Arc insisted on as being the only place for the coronation of Charles VII, and it was here in 1429 in the Cathedral of Reims that Charles VII was crowned King of France. Ever since the baptism of Clovis by Saint Rémi in 498-9, it has been the traditional site for the coronation of the French kings. Adding to the cathedral's importance is the famous Smiling Angel, symbol of Reims, at the west front of the cathedral. Also in Reims is the beautiful Basilique of Saint Rémi. Not too far away is another beautiful cathedral at Soissons. In fact, France is full of beautiful cathedrals, most of them Gothic in style.

While I was at Reims, I got to see the Bastille Day celebration, July 14, similar to our 4th of July celebration, but with much more hoopla. It all begins on the eve of the 13th with neighborhood dances until the wee hours of the morning. Then there is always a parade down the main street of the city. I remember my first Bastille Day in 1963 in Paris. A group of girls went up to the Place de la Concorde to witness the parade. In order to see better, we got up and stood on the stone balusters surrounding the Place. While we were concentrating on the parade, an enterprising

Frenchman capitalized on the situation by sliding a mirror along the stone balusters allowing him an excellent view of the girls' legs and under garments. When I saw him doing this, I screamed at my friends, "Someone's looking up our skirts", and he immediately disappeared. That was a unique situation, and I never saw this repeated in any more French celebrations. Also this manoeuvre would not be likely today since very few of the girls ever wear skirts. So that guy would be put out of business with the popularity of slacks and jeans.

While at the university, we had many visits to the nearby wine "caves" where the champagne is stored. The nearby city of Epernay is the heart of the Champagne country. It is considered the main entrepôt for champagne wines, so we had many tours to the Epernay "caves" accompanied by many taste experiences. I remember visits to Moët & Chandon and Mercier, in Epernay. Reims also had its share of caves to visit such as Charles Heidsieck, Taittinger, Mumm, and Piper-Heidsieck. After classes, we had a variety of caves to visit.

France has never been very good at providing good toilet facilities. The restaurants in the cities always had one room, usually downstairs, or at the back, devoted to one toilet. But for the men on the street, France eventually provided a "pissoir" which was an open-air gazebo-like building, which they could use. (Photo #21)

Photo #21

But sometimes the men didn't use the "pissoir". Instead they just stopped along the street, found the corner of a building, turned their back to the public and relieved themselves. Sometimes in the large cities the toilet facilities were just short of adequate, but in the villages, they were less than adequate. The usual toilet was in a small room with 2 elevated footprints on which to stand. Then when finished, you pulled a chain on the wall, and a cascade of water swirled around your feet. If you did find a flushing toilet, you could see many, many ways to flush. A book could be written on the astronomical different ways to flush the French toilet. I can remember my 1963 French trip. Many of the French restaurants even in Paris didn't have modern plumbing. They had a girl with a bucket of water who would flush the footprints when you had finished. Now that's a job that you couldn't give away today.

Today horsemeat is no longer considered a staple; however in 1966, it was very common to see horsemeat sold in stores in and around the cities of France. (Photo #22) The shop may have been labeled "chevaline", or it very likely had a golden horse head outside to advertise its wares. I never wanted to eat horsemeat, but in the cafeterias at the universities, you never really knew what you were eating.

Photo #22

When our studies were finished at the University of Reims, our study group continued our tour. Our first stop was Orléans, then Nevers, a small village where the body of Sainte Bernadette can be viewed in the small Convent of St. Gildard. (Photo #23)

Photo #23

Years later while traveling with my students through France, we found ourselves in Nevers for a lunch stop. I immediately gathered my 8 students around me and headed for the St. Gildard Convent. When the Mother Superior answered the door, I spoke to her in French and asked her if we could view the body of Ste. Bernadette. I told her we were from Ohio, and that we only had a little time to spend, but she graciously open the door for us and let us view the intact body of Ste. Bernadette. That was a once-in-a-lifetime experience for my group. We grabbed a sandwich on the run and got on the bus in time, but we had a really memorable experience.

After Never we toured Limoges, Toulouse, and the beautiful walled city of Carcassonne, then on to Marseilles where the statue of Notre Dame de la Garde protects the fishermen of Marseilles as they leave and return to port. From Marseilles you can see the prison-fortress of Château d'If, made famous when Alexandre Dumas used it as his setting for <u>The Count of Monte Cristo</u>. From Marseilles we drove to the port of Toulon and Nice. From there we turned northward through the Alps to Grenoble, then to Geneva and Lake Léman or sometimes called Lake Geneva. On the northern shore of the lake is the Château de Chillon. It was made popular by Lord Byron in the poem, *The Prisoner of Chillon*. We toured the castle and viewed the dungeon in which Lord Byron had scrawled his name. From Geneva we returned to Paris for a flight home.

Chapter Six

1967 Travcoa 70-Day Around the World Kipling Tour

Now that I found out that I could live many days out of a suitcase, I decided to expand it to 70 days. My trip of choice was Travcoa's 70-Day Trip Around the World. So with 2 hardback Samsonite suitcases and a small flight bag, I packed for the next 70 days. The trip began June 9, 1967, and ended August 17. I chose the Travcoa Escorted Round the World Kipling Tour. Oh, was travel different then. There were no security lines. The airlines gave us great service and food. They actually made us feel welcome. Many times the food was gourmet. We had lots of room on the planes because they were only partially full. For our trip we stayed at Deluxe and First Class Hotels. Three meals a day was included on à la carte basis. We could eat our meals in any of the hotels' upscale restaurants. It was not uncommon to have dinner on the top floor of the hotel in the Skyline Room where we could overlook the city.

My 70 day trip cost $1,995.00 for the land portion + $1,375.00 for the airfare for a total of $3,370.00. The price included sightseeing with English-speaking guides, entrances fees, and gratuities to hotel staff. We did, however, have to pay for our passport, laundry, drinks, and items of a personal nature. Of course, $3,370.00 was a lot of money in 1967, almost a year's teachers' salary. I had such a stack of plane tickets that the Delta staff at the Cincinnati Airport was in stitches when they saw them. My plane tickets included the following: Cincinnati, Chicago, San Francisco, Honolulu, Tokyo, Osaka, Taipei, Manila, Hong Kong, Phnom Penh, Seim Reap, Bangkok, Singapore, Colombo, Madras, Calcutta, Kathmandu, Patna, Banaras, Agra, New Delhi, Srinagar, Amritsar, Lahore, Peshawar, Kabul, Teheran, Isfahan, Teheran, Beirut, Cairo, Luxor, Cairo, Jerusalem, Tel Aviv, Istanbul, Athens, New York, Cincinnati.

So my trip consisted of more than 30 flights plus a lot of surface travel. Surface travel was by minivans or private cars since we were a small group of 10 travelers. Upon arriving in the foreign cities, we were each given a package containing the itinerary for that particular country. Travel today is so expensive that a 70-day trip would be out of sight, and it would never include 3 à la carte meals.

June 9. We left the Greater Cincinnati airport at 3:30 P.M. on a Delta flight bound for Chicago. Our plane was delayed, and my luggage missed the American flight to San Francisco. Since I had a 3-hour layover in S.F., there was enough time for my luggage to catch up with me. The total time from S.F. to Honolulu was 5 hours, and the total time from Cincinnati to Honolulu was 15 hours. When we arrived in Honolulu, we each received a yellow Plumeria Lei. Plumeria is also called Frangipani. Our hotel was the Ilikai, and our room overlooked the harbor. Not much was seen in Honolulu because it was just a stopover en route to Japan. We did, however, have a view of Diamondhead in the distance. An overnight in Hawaii helped break up a very long flight.

June 10. Our next flight would be from Honolulu to Tokyo and would last 8 hours. Before leaving Honolulu, I loaded up on American cigarettes at the Duty Free Shop. A carton cost $2.25. At that time, I was a smoker just like many of my friends. In 1967 little attention was paid to the damage that could be done by cigarettes. The next day we crossed the International Date Line, and we all got a certificate with the particulars.

June 12. Our arrival in Japan was enhanced by a view of the sun glittering over Mr. Fujiyama. We would be spending 7 days in Japan. Our stay at Tokyo would be at the Imperial Hotel. Our guide in Japan was Toshi. During our sightseeing tour of the city we saw the famous Ginza Shopping Center and passed the Shinto Shrine with Torii Gates, which purify you as you pass. In the evening the group went to a Kabuki theater to see a one-hour dance and then a play. Spectators shouted during the entire performance. People ate and drank during the play. Then we visited a place called Victor's Pearls before returning to the hotel for dinner.

June 13. The next morning we took a train to Nikko. Our trip lasted 1 hour 45 minutes, and we passed many rice patties. When we arrived, we checked into the Kanaya Hotel and had lunch. Since our guide Toshi was vice president of the Japan Travel Bureau, he was always giving us bits and pieces of Japanese history and culture. In the afternoon there was time for shopping before visiting the famous Shinto shrine—Toshogu Shrine with a 5-story pagoda. Drums are a positive symbol like birth. Bells are a negative symbol like death. Countless woodcarvings and large amounts of gold leaf were used to decorate the buildings in a way not seen elsewhere in Japan, where simplicity has been traditionally stressed. The shrine is situated in a beautiful forest and is a combination of Buddhism and Shintoism. The buildings are decorated with gold leaf used to enhance the woodcarvings. Slips of paper with bad fortunes were placed in trees. I can only imagine that was to divert any impending bad luck. We took off our shoes to enter the outer sanctuary and walked on Tatami Mats 3' X 6'. All rooms are measured by the size of the Tatami Mats, either 6' or 9'. Only priests are allowed in the center and inner sanctuary. Later we drove to Kegon Waterfall and then along Lake Chuzenji. We stopped at Dragonhead Falls. As an added feature we visited a Samari warrior's house where we were served sweet cookies and green tea with salt. Our Japanese hostess sang 3 songs for us. A Japanese family plants a Pawlonic Tree at a daughter's birth, and this is made into a chest of drawers when she marries. Later we returned to the hotel for dinner and a Japanese movie.

June 14. The next morning after breakfast at the Kanaya Hotel, we returned to Tokyo by train. We visited another shrine where a feudal lord had planted 40,000 cedar trees 300 years ago. Now only 16,000 remain. We also learned several Japanese customs. Pedestrians carry yellow banners and wave them as they cross the street. Cattle are fed beer and rubbed down with Shochu (white liquor) and massaged with a straw rope. Drinking beer makes the cows eat more. Massage disperses the fat. Almost 90% of Tokyo was destroyed during the war. Commuter trains employ "pushers" for rush hours. They would push the commuters into the cars. They found this method ineffective so they decided to employ "pullers, pulling people out while saying, "Take the next train." Young girls employed as "pullers" can expect to find their "falsies" on their back after this procedure.

The middle of June to the middle of July is the rainy season in Japan. Eighty percent of the tea grown is green tea. Twenty percent is black tea. The tealeaf is the same only black in color. No sugar is added to green tea when it is served. Tea is considered good for strengthening the veins and preventing cerebral hemorrhages.

We arrived in Tokyo and had lunch at the Imperial Hotel in the Viking Restaurant. Then we had some leisure time. Our itinerary then included a trip to a flower arranging school where we went to see how the Japanese perfect this art. The Japanese don't just bunch the flowers into a vase. They choose each flower separately so that it is shown to its best advantage. In the evening we went to the Matsubaya Restaurant and had a Sukiyaki dinner—thin strips of beef, sliced green onions, carrots, and soybean curd. It must be eaten with rice and be dipped in a beaten raw egg. Sake wine accompanies most meals. Sake is always served hot. The floorshow included more Geisha girls. Of course, our shoes were left at the door of the restaurant.

June 15. The following morning after breakfast, we passed Yokohama on our 40-mile trip to Kamakura to see the Great Buddha. It was cast in 1252 and made of bronze. Cast in 8 parts, it is the second largest in Japan, the largest being in Nari. This one was pictured in the film *Around the World in 80 days*. We had lunch at the Hayama Marina. On our return we passed Picture Island and Shonan Beach. We arrived at the Fujiya Hotel in Miyanoshita, a small resort town famous for its hot baths. The hotel gardens were magnificent. That evening after dinner, I treated myself to a massage in my room. The massage was done by a woman and cost $1.70 plus a $.60 tip.

June 16. The next morning in Miyanoshita we took a 2-1/2 mile cable car ride over the hot springs and Hakone Crater. We exited the cable car at Lake Hakone. Lunch was at the Hakone Hotel. Later we crossed Lake Hakone in a Viking ship. Then we took the world's fastest train to Kyoto, the 5th largest city in Japan with 1 million, 300 thousand inhabitants. Even on the fastest train, it was a 3-hour ride to Kyoto.

We checked in to the Kyoto Hotel where we had dinner. Kyoto has 500 Shinto shrines. Nara and Kyoto are considered the cradle of Japanese culture and civilization. Thanks to an American advisor on Japanese culture, neither city was bombed during the war. Here I learned that Shinto have shrines and Buddhist have temples.

June 17. After breakfast we set out on a 3-hour sightseeing tour, which included a visit to Nijo Castle, which was built in 1603. It was built for a Shogun as a fortress. We also visited the Golden Pavilion, the summer residence of a Shogun, now a Buddhist Temple belonging to the Zen Sect. We shopped at Oridono Silk Center and visited the Ikenobo Flower Arranging School. Then we returned to the hotel for lunch. Afterwards we had some free time. In the evening after dinner, I went to see the Cormorant Fishing, a very interesting procedure. Each of the Cormorant Birds is attached on a string. The fisherman beats on the side of the boat to encourage the birds. The boat is equipped with a large light or burning pine strips which are employed in order to attract the fish. An experienced fisherman can handle 12 birds at once. The birds all grab the fish but because of a string around their throat, they cannot swallow the fish. When the Cormorant catches a fish, the fisherman pulls it up and takes its prey out of its mouth. The Cormorant just thinks it has caught its dinner. Most of the fish caught are trout. The tour cost an additional $4.20.

There are some festivals in Japan. The Girls' Festival is March 3. Then the girls display their doll collection. This is not a National Holiday. Then April 2, a national holiday, is the Emperor's Birthday. Labor Day is May 1, but it is not a national holiday. Constitution Day is May 3. There is also a Boys Festival on May 5.

Japan is noted for its cultural pearl industry. Oysters are opened, and an irritant is implanted in the oyster. Muscle shells are imported from Mississippi, and these are ground and served as irritants. The irritant is implanted when the oysters are 3 years old. Oysters are suspended from a raft, and they are taken inland to the southern seas during winter. Luster for a pearl is all-important. A pearl oyster is not edible, and the oyster must be killed in order to extract its treasure. Mikimoto Pearls are considered the best in the world. A pink pearl is the most desired, but color cannot be controlled. During the pearl making process, the oysters are cleaned of their barnacles every 2 months. Spherical shapes are much in demand. The oyster usually has 1 or 2 flaws, and it is here that the holes are drilled. Ninety-five percent of the pearls are no-good. Only five percent are put on the market.

The bus tours in Japan are interesting. The roads are terrible; however the buses are air-conditioned, but antiquated. Each bus has a Japanese hostess who sings in her spare time when tourists get bored. She will also blow a whistle when the bus is backing up. Pedestrians crossing the street carry yellow flags to signal their presence.

June 18. In Kyoto I did get to attend a Catholic Mass. It was at 6:30 A.M. and was conducted by the Maryknoll Fathers. After breakfast, our group left the hotel for a 4-hour sightseeing tour of Nara, about 45 minutes away by bus. Nara was the capital from 710-784. There is a Great Buddha in Deer Park or Nara Park. The deer are sacred in Japan. They are considered divine messengers. We all bought packages of rice cakes from the street venders so that we could feed the deer. Strangely enough, the deer ignore the rice cakes on the venders' stands, but immediately after purchase, the deer crowd around the buyer. They pushed me and nibbled my dress. One deer was so enthusiastic about eating that it jumped up on me and scratched my arm. The deer will imitate you if you bow. Some will bow on command. One followed me all the way down the path walking by my side. The 1,000 deer are running free among the tourists. They are cared for by the city and are penned up at night. (Photo #24)

Photo #24

The Kasuga Shrine has 3,000 lanterns. Also, and more important in the park is the Great Buddha which was cast in 749. Only the lotus flower foundation is original. The Buddha represents a preaching style with the right hand giving peace of mind and the left hand answering wishes.

Shintoism is older than Buddhism. It has many Kamis or gods, some 8 million gods. The Goddess of the Sun is the center. She is the ancestress of the imperial family. Ancestral worship is important in this religion along with hero worship. Many Shinto shrines are dedicated to great men. Ordinary men become Buddhas. Great men become Gods. There is a worship of nature like the God of the Mountain and the God of Water. The Torii gate is the symbol of Shintoism. Shintoism began losing popularity after the war. The militarists utilized the influence of the Emperor. It is nationalistic and stresses obedience to war.

Buddhism was founded in India in the 5th century B.C. It stresses Buddhahood as a state of perfection, free of suffering. We cannot be perfect, but we must try. There are 108 desires, and a bell is rung 108 times on New Year's Eve to get rid of these 108 desires. Buddha means enlightened one. Everyone is a Buddha after death. There are 2 main schools in this religion—northern Buddhism and southern Buddhism. Northern Buddhism is a milder form and came to Japan via Korea. It is tolerant, flexible and compatible with Shintoism. Southern Buddhism is strict with no compromise. It is found in Burma and Thailand and includes fasting. Japan belongs to the northern school, which is more liberal. There are many sects after the Reformation including Zen, which was born in India and preached in China. Zen tries to attain perfection by means of contemplation. No idol helps you attain this perfection. It is a kind of atheism, and it is more like ethics.

Returning to Kyoto after the trip to Nara, we had lunch and then left for a Tea Ceremony in a private home. We removed our shoes at the doorway, and the guests sat on pillows on Tatami Mats.

There are 4 points of a tea ceremony: harmony, respect, cleanliness, and quietness. The tea ceremony was started by a Zen Priest in China. It cultivates mental composure. Girls of good families study this ceremony, along with flower arranging, while they are growing up. It was established in the 14th century. The tea ceremony can never be repeated in time or space. We should recognize our existence time-wise and space-wise. It is based on Zen Buddhism and Japanese philosophy. Green powdered tea is used with no sugar. The cup is turned twice and then is given to the guest who also will turn the cup twice. Cakes were served and eaten before the tea arrives.

After the tea ceremony, the mother arranged flowers in both a traditional and a modern way. Three items must be present in both forms—heaven, man, and earth. Leaves are used for the traditional method, and flowers are used for the modern design. The flowers should resemble nature and should be displayed exactly in the way that they grow. After the flower ceremony, the hostess's daughter performed two dances, one with a fan and the other with a parasol. A record player supplied the music. Then the daughter played the Koto Harp, a type of guitar. The Michelangelo of Japanese flowers arranging is a man called Sofu. He has founded a school of flower arranging In Tokyo called Sogetsu, and he has published a beautiful book on the subject called simply SOFU.

Our trip is now getting ready to travel to Taiwan. However, before leaving Japan, I wanted to remember some impressions of this country. Hiroshige is famous for wood block prints. Van Gogh and Monet copied his work. Sumi Art is popular using Indian ink. The greatest Sumi art painter is Seshu. Haiku features short little Japanese poems. Baslo is the greatest of Haiku artists. Haiku always has 17 syllables in Japanese, divided 5-7-5. In translation it is usually longer. And it is always about the four seasons such as—Cricket Song, in a Spring Garden, Silent Fire Fly, or A Net of Fire Flies. This country opened my eyes to a unique culture that I never knew existed. The Japanese people were so hospital and so eager to show off their country.

June 19. We left the Kyoto Hotel at 8:30 A.M. and headed towards Taiwan. Our hotel had a large Sayonara Sign—We'll see you again. We took a bus to the Osaka Airport for our flight to Taipei with Thai international. The plane and crew belonged to Thailand, but the hostesses were Japanese. We really got the royal treatment on the plane—cold towels, orchids, a fan, juice, cigarettes, magazines, hors d'oeuvres, salmon, chicken and rice, vegetables, red wine, dessert, beer, coffee and tea, more cigarettes, then a glass of coke.

Mainland China was closed at this time to tourists, so the only Chinese country open to tourists was the island of Taiwan. The flight lasted 2 hours, 40 minutes at an altitude of 25,000 feet. We lost one hour in time, however. Taipei was about 15-20 degrees warmer than Tokyo.

After customs we checked into the Grand Hotel in Taipei, the most elegant hotel in the city. All the V.I.P.'s stayed here including Eisenhower, Nixon, and Johnson. The hotel is "bugged" for communist Chinese. The Grand Hotel is the best example of Chinese architecture around. The afternoon was spent in city sightseeing including the National Palace Museum or Chung Shan Palace Museum. There are many valuable artifacts to see here such as bronzes, dating back two centuries before Christ, 14th century silk and paper paintings, both Ming and Ch'ing dynasty carvings, and porcelains.

There are three groups in Taiwan: the Taiwanese who are of Chinese ancestry, Indians who are aborigines (the original inhabitants), and the Chinese who came in the 1940's. There is no physical difference between the Taiwanese and the Chinese. However the southern Chinese are smaller than the Northern Chinese who are taller and bigger. The average wage per month is $20.00-$25.00. There are not many cars. But there are ox carts and pedicabs, which have 3 wheels and are very much like our bicycles, but with a compartment for carrying passengers.

The Chinese are not very religious, according to our guide. Educated people follow Confucius' teachings and are agnostic. The uneducated say that they are Buddhist, but it's really the superstition, which appeals to them. From 1895 until 1945 this island was under Japanese rule. Taiwan has 6 years of compulsory education. After that the parents must pay.

Our second stop was the Confucius Shrine followed by a beautiful Buddhist Temple, Lungshan Temple. Confucius lived 551 B. C. Our fourth stop was a Cathay Handicraft Center where we bought souvenirs and had them shipped home. That evening we left for a Mongolian Barbeque at riverside. We had our choice of 4 kinds of meat: beef, wild boar, venison, or mutton. It was served with cabbage, carrots, onions, tomatoes, udo, parsley, sesame seed oil, soy sauce and all kinds of salad oils and hot peppers. Udo is a Japanese vegetable in the ginseng family, which looks a lot like asparagus. All the ingredients are put into a bowl, and the chef pours everything on a flaming grill for about 2 minutes. It's eaten with chopsticks and served with cold rice wine which tastes like sake. We also had hot Jasmine Tea and rice soup. To cleanse our palate we were served slices of watermelon. Incense was burned in beer bottles and put on the ground around the tables. The local boys took lots of pictures of us and distributed them later at the hotel for $.50 each.

June 20. The next morning after a fruit breakfast, we boarded a bus for the Wulai Aborigine Village. The ride lasted about 1 hour, 20 minutes. After the bus we took a pushcart going uphill to reach the village. We photographed the native girls and were treated to a beautiful waterfall. Then we descended halfway for Wulai dancing. The show lasted 45 minutes and featured marriage rites, rice harvesting, illness in the family, and events meaningful to the aborigines. Then it was time to return to the hotel for lunch so we descended again via pushcarts to the bus. I bought a coke later and paid 10 NT (New Taiwan) dollars, about 25 cents in our money. That afternoon I was not feeling well, and the tour director called a local doctor who came to the hotel to see me. Not knowing exactly my problem, he decided to give me a vitamin shot.

June 21. In the morning after breakfast I returned to the Cathay Handicraft Center for shopping. In the afternoon we left the hotel at 5:00 P.M. and took a bus to the airport. Our guide, T.C., saw us off. The plane left at 6:55 P.M., and the flight lasted 1-1/2 hours. Our flight was a C.A.T. (Civil Air Transport) Flight to Manila. It was a beautiful plane. Customs, on the other hand, was a nightmare. There were many Chinese aboard who had to pay an immigration fee. When we did get past the line, we were presented with a beautiful Jasmine Lei. The little bus to the hotel was air-conditioned, but the Manila Hotel was old and dreary. It's the best in Manila, but the best is none too good. There were several shops in the hotel, but the windows were filthy. Lucky for us, the following day was busy with things to see so little time would be spent in the room. Our guide was Rudy. Two new hotels are being built but will not be finished until the following year: the Sheraton Hotel and the Hilton Hotel.

Manila has two million people and was under Spanish occupation from 1571-1819. We visited St. Augustine Church, the 2nd oldest in Asia. It is on a floating foundation, and the ceiling gives the effect of sculpture. Before the Spanish, Manila was under Moslem rule. The pineapple is the symbol of the Moslems. Legaspi is considered the founder of Manila. He died August 21, 1572, and is buried in Saint Augustine Church. The bell of Saint Augustine was cast in Seville. At the time of my trip, 93% of the people were Christian, and 7% were Moslems

Manila is the 2nd most destroyed city during W.W. II after Warsaw. The Japanese bombed it and used it as a concentration camp. Twenty-two thousand Americans and Filipinos died during the 3-year Japanese occupation. Dr. José Rizal was the greatest Filipino statesman, and the Spanish executed him at the age of 35 in 1896. Rizal wrote "My Last Farewell". Manila is named after a flower.

Its educational system is patterned after the U.S. system with 6 years of compulsory schooling and 4 years of high school, which must be paid by the parents ($27.00 a year). The teachers' salary is $100.00 a month for 8 months. Buses are replaced by jeepneys 8-10 capacity. They look like jeeps. Gas is 27¢ a gallon. Quezon is the real capital of the Philippines, but most of the business is transacted in Manila. English is the language of business. There are many dialects in the Filipino language.

There appeared to be lots of slums in Manila. Its most modern suburb is Makati. There are 11,207 graves in the Manila American Cemetery: 60% American 40% Filipino. We stopped at a Filipino restaurant, but I was not enamored with the selection. In fact, I was repulsed at what they ate. Their delicacies include goat meat, python, iguanas, and 21-day-old duck eggs called baluts. The eggs are almost ready to hatch. Fruit bats are also a delicacy and dog meat is more expensive than beef.

June 22. We stopped to see the famous bamboo organ at Las Pinas Rival. The organ is 146 years old, and the church is 200 years old. Later we stopped at Taal Crater Lake. We then visited a private home built on stilts because of floods and because it is good for ventilation. Later we had another visit, this time to the home of Dr. and Mrs. Enriquez. She is the head of the Manila Travel Agency. She served us rice cakes, coconut, and ice tea. The daughter and several cousins all fanned us and kept the flies away. The neighborhood kids came running in a stampede to shake hands and say hello. Later we returned to Manila and passed many oyster beds and salt beds on our way back to the hotel. The salt beds are used as fish hatcheries. Cock fighting is the national pastime in the country. The national pastime in the city is Jaialai.

June 23. The next morning on the way to the airport I couldn't help but notice slogans and names written all over the buildings and fences. We left Manila on PAL Philippine Airlines and flew at an altitude of 35,000 feet to Hong Kong. The flight lasted about 1-1/2 hours. There is a one-hour time difference. Our planned trip to Macao got cancelled due to difficulties there. We arrived at the Peninsula Hotel and checked in to a very luxurious room (202) with wall-to-wall carpeting and 2 phones, 1 of which was in the carpeted bathroom. The bathroom has 2 basins, 2 showers and a tub. There were lots of buttons to push and mirrors galore. A vase of orchids was waiting in our room as well as a basket of fruit

There are 4 million people in Hong Kong all in 20 square miles. The New Territories are leased, and the lease expired in 1998. There are 4 major problems in Hong Kong. Water is the first. Supply must depend on the rainfall. Second is the 150,000 floating population. The third is that there is no compulsory education. The fourth is that there are very few doctors and hospitals, only outpatient clinics. They also have another problem. Eighty percent are narcotic addicts. There is a Bamboo Curtain here, and the river is the boundary line. Tourists are not allowed to go to the border since telephoto lenses were employed a few years ago.

June 24. We had a whole day of shopping due to the cancellation of our Macao trip. In the afternoon I visited the Man Hing Ivory Factory and purchased an Ivory hand carved ball with17 balls inside all standing on an elephant stand. I paid $50.00 for it plus $1.00 for a C.C.O. (Comprehensive Certificate of Origin). The C.C.O. was necessary to get the ivory past U.S. customs. There were many ivory selections to choose from in the Man Hing Ivory Factory Catalogue. (Photo #25)

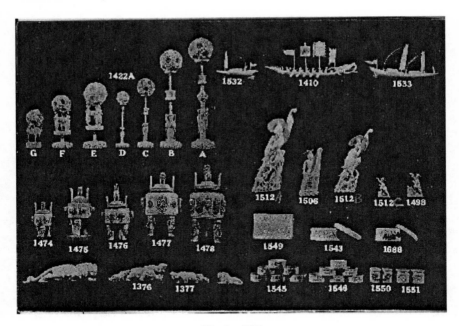

Photo #25

June 25. The next morning we had breakfast in the Veranda Room. Then there was sightseeing on Hong Kong Island. Afterwards we took the Star Ferry across Victoria Bay or Victoria Harbor. Then we took the Peak Tram Cable Car (funicular) to the top of the hill which is 1,305 feet above sea level. From there Kowloon Peninsula can be seen. Kowloon means 9 dragons or mountains. Later we visited Tiger Balm Gardens, which was constructed in 1935 by Mr. A.W. Boon Haw at a cost of 16 million H.K. dollars. He actually earned his money by smuggling, not by the sale of Tiger Balm. Lunch was at the Repulse Bay Hotel, which is a branch of the Peninsula Hotel. The view of the bay from the terrace was excellent. Later we rode to Aberdeen, Hong Kong's main fishing village. We returned to the hotel for dinner after a Star Ferry Ride.

June 26. The next morning I went shopping again and bought a Tiger's Eye Buddha Charm, 1 carton of Viceroys for $2.25, and another ivory concentric ball, which I sent to my mother. In the evening we took a sunset cruise of the South China Sea to replace the missed trip to Macao. Dinner was on a floating restaurant—The Sea Palace in Aberdeen. We had several courses of Chinese food. We returned to the hotel after a tour of Victoria Harbor.

June 27. In the morning I checked in with the hotel doctor and received another vitamin shot. For dinner we took a rickshaw ride to the Ocean Terminal where we had Chinese food in the Night Club Oceania. The meal had 10 courses plus tea. We saw 2 different floorshows. I liked the ribbon dance the best. We ate from 8:00 P.M. until 11:00 P.M.

June 28. The following morning we flew from Hong Kong to Siem Reap, Cambodia. Our airline was RAC—Royal Air Cambodge, and the flight lasted 3-1/2 hours to Phnom Penh. Then we had a 50-minute layover before continuing to Siem Reap. Dinner was at the Grand Hotel D'Angkor. Our room was beautiful but was infested with giant crickets. They were attracted to the light. We also had a lizard in our bath. My roommate and I put a blotter under the balcony door and a floor mat under the bath door to keep out the pests.

June 29. The next morning after breakfast we left for Bayon Temple at Angkor Thom, built in 1181. (Photo #26) After returning to the hotel for lunch, we toured Angkor Wat, a temple dedicated to the Brahmin god Vishnu, the protector. It was built in 1112 as a funeral temple, and it covers 3-1/2 square miles. This temple is a contemporary to Notre Dame in Paris and to the cathedral of Chartres. These

800-year-old ruins of Angkor Wat are one of the world's great archeological wonders. We climbed the steepest steps ever, and then returned to the hotel. I was glad to see these wonderful ruins before some radical tries to blow them up.

Photo #26

Later I took a ride in a cyclo-pousses or tricycle-rickshaws. Cost was $1.00 for 1 hour or 35 Riels in Cambodian money. We toured the village of Siem Reap where there were people bathing nude in the river.

June 30. After breakfast the next morning we left Siem Reap early and flew via Royal Air Cambodge to Phnom Penh. It was only a 1-hour flight. We had a 3-hour layover at Phnom Penh so we decided to take an optional sightseeing tour for $3.00. We toured the National Museum and the Royal Palace. Our plane to Bangkok on Air Vietnam Caravelle was a little late, but they treated us royally;

however it was very bumpy. Our lunch was Russian Tomato with sausages, then cold spring chicken in jelly, roast beef, then pastries. The lunch was written on a menu with a silk cover. That was very impressive. Upon arrival at the Siam Intercontinental I went swimming, followed by shopping, and dinner, which consisted of a sea food salad, cream soup, beef, potatoes, salad, and orange sherbet. It was served in the Leopard Room with an orchestra and a singer.

Afterwards we left to see Thai Classical Dancing at the Rama Hotel. They performed 11 numbers. It is the Forum School of Dancing and was recommended by the Hilton Management. There was an announcer to explain each of the dances. One even included an authentic wedding ceremony. The Forum School of Dancing is a unique program and the only place in Bangkok where Thai Cultures, Folk Dancing, and Classical Dancing are presented.

July 1. The next morning in Bangkok, we left the hotel early at 7:00 A.M. for a tour of the unusual Floating Market up the Chao Phya River. The markets float right in front of the many homes along the river. Then we turned into a canal where everyone throws his garbage. We passed several floating dead dogs, then stopped to see Thai silk being woven. Our boat got stuck at the Silk Factory so we had to wait until the high tide arrived before we could leave. Even then we still couldn't move so we had to walk through part of the jungle. The boat picked us up later. Then we visited the Royal Barges and the Temple of Dawn. This morning excursion lasted 6 hours. Then we returned to the hotel for lunch and a mini nap.

At 5:30 we went to see Thai boxing. First Row seats cost us $5.00 each. The Lumpinee Stadium advertises as the only boxing stadium that has never disappointed its audiences. There were 8 events or matches, each consisting of 5 rounds. Seven of the events demonstrated Thai Boxing Style. One of the events used the International Style, and it was the Featured Event. The names of each boxer was listed along with his Boxing Camp, his weight in pounds, and the corner of the ring, either red or blue, which was his. So the program was very easy to follow. Thai boxing differs from American boxing. They put on gloves, but in addition to using their hands, they may also use their knees, and legs. Thai music is played during each 3 minute round. At the beginning, each boxer says his prayers and faces his native village. Although each bout lasts only for 5 rounds, it is stopped if one of the fighters is knocked out. Bleeding does not stop the fight if it is below the eye. We watched 7 out of the 8 rounds. The main event was International just like our own boxing. However, it was stopped in the 3rd round due to bleeding. We returned to the hotel before the 8th round. We had seen enough.

July 2. The next morning early I went to a 7:00 mass, and at 9:00 we left for our sightseeing tour of the Palace of Kings, the Marble Temple, then to the Temple of the Emerald (Jade) Buddha, then to the Temple of the Golden Buddha. Since it began to rain, we postponed our tour of the Reclining Buddha until the afternoon. We had lunch at the hotel. Then we headed for the airport. On the way, we stopped at the Reclining Buddha. We caught the 7:00 P.M. flight to Singapore on Thai International. The flight took 2 hours and

15 minutes at an altitude of 29,000 feet. There is also a ½ hour time difference between Thailand and Singapore.

I learned several things about Singapore. It is 26 miles long, and 14 miles wide. Chinese coolies all wear royal blue, and their pay is $1.50 for a 7-hour day. Singapore has banned Playboy Magazine, rock-n-roll, and slot machines. All citizens over the age of 31 are required to vote or face a fine or imprisonment. Tiger Balm Gardens cost 1 million dollars.

July 3. We stopped at the Tiger Oil House of Jade, which is owned by the man who built Tiger Balm Garden. We also toured the Botanical Gardens, the famous Haw Par Jade Collection, and fed the monkeys. Then we were off for a drive across the island past rubber plantations to the Sultanate of Johore. Later we returned to the Raffles Hotel and were surprised to find our names imprinted on the hotel stationery in our rooms. This is the hotel popularized by Somerset Maugham when he wrote that the Raffles Hotel stood "for all the fables of the exotic East". In truth, this hotel is unique. It is the oldest, biggest, and best of Singapore's hotels. The hotel owes its name to Sir Stamford Raffles who was important to the establishment of Singapore. Dinner at the Raffles Regency Room included filet mignon, french-fries, and pistachio ice cream.

July 4. The next morning we were up at 4:30 A.M. to catch a B.O.A.C. flight to Colombo, Ceylon. We were on a DC 10, and we made one stop at Kuala Lumpur because our hydraulic brakes were leaking. This was a 3-hour flight with a 2-hour time change. Because we were going to overnight in Kandy, we were asked to leave our main suitcase in the hands of the airport porters and only take a small overnight bag to Kandy. We would rendezvous with our main suitcase the following day. Then we had a 3-hour bus ride to Kandy, the capital of Ceylon. The country seems very poor, and the men wear G-strings while working in the fields. The Queen's hotel is very bleak. We saw thousands of crows, and we visited a Buddhist Temple where they beat drums and play a flute. We saw the Temple, which contains the sacred Tooth Relic of Lord Buddha, perhaps the most venerated shrine in Ceylon. There the white clad worshippers offer sweet scented jasmine and lotus and pay homage to the Enlightened One. There are elephants in the street outside the hotel. For dinner we had a huge avocado fixed with vinegar and oil and salt and pepper. This is the 4th of July, but there are no celebrations. For entertainment the Kandyan dancers performed.

July 5. The next morning we left Kandy at 8:30 A.M. and drove to the Botanical Gardens. There we saw nutmeg trees, allspice trees, and beautiful orchids. En route to Columbo we stopped on the road and set off 3 rockets to scare the fruit bats, which were hanging upside down on the trees. Later we stopped at a tea factory where they make orange pekoe tea, then to the Galle Face Hotel in Colombo.

(Photo #27)

When I rendezvoused with my major suitcase, I was greatly upset because the B.O.A.C. airport boys had stolen all two cartons of my Viceroy cigarettes from my suitcase when they transferred the suitcases to the Galle Face Hotel in Colombo. That left me with no cigarettes. So the remainder of the trip I would have to smoke the strong Turkish cigarettes or the equally strong French Gauloises. What a dilemma! That night we had dinner in the Rathskeller of the hotel—filet mignon, salad, and coupe Jacques. Afterwards my roommate and I went walking on the beach outside the hotel. The moon was out and the ocean was beautiful. We wandered a little ways down the coast, then put our purses down, and sat down to enjoy the ambiance of the moonlight on the Indian Ocean. Not long afterwards, the hotel security came after us and escorted us back to the hotel beach. It seems that we had wandered onto the public beach in our moonlight stroll, and the public beach was not safe. Only the private beach in front of the hotel was guarded. When we looked around us, we could see the natives inching closer and closer to where we were sitting. Of course, we were not thinking of danger, we were enamored with the ambiance of Ceylon. I am glad that the hotel was watching out for us. A local mugging would have really ruined the trip. Our guide, Dave, is seeking reimbursement for my lost cigarettes from our local guide Eustace.

July 6. The next morning we got up very early at 4:30 to catch our 7:30 flight to Madras only to find out that it was an afternoon flight. The flight took us over the Bay of Bengal. When we finally got to the Imperial Hotel in Madras, we found it very like an American motel. In the afternoon we toured Madras with 2 Indian guides dressed in sarees.

Some facts that I learned about Madras and its inhabitants are: Dobee's are men who wash clothes on rocks by the river. Sikhs from the Punjab area do not shave ever. They are a cross between Muslin and Hindu. This religion was to strengthen Hinduism. Poperdum is like a large exploded potato chip. Curry (hot) is their main dish. Dhothi is a long white dress that can be shortened by pulling it up. Jains are a branch of Hinduism who sweeps the sidewalk in front of them so they will not step on any insects. They wear masks in the temple so they won't inhale any insects. The emperors encouraged the mughal paintings. Married women all wear beads given to them by their husbands. The old fashioned ones wear nose rings similar to the earrings that are for pierced ears. They all wear spots on their foreheads.

Most sarees are 6 yards long. Teenagers start wearing the half saree (3 yards) at about 12-13 years old.

In Madras we visited the National Art Gallery, Fort St. George, and St. Thomas Cathedral where St. Thomas was buried. We also visited Mylapore Hindu Temple where services were being conducted. We had to take off our shoes and watch out for cow dung on the floor. There was the local snake charmer in front of the temple. Later we returned to the Imperial Hotel for dinner.

July 7. The next afternoon we flew via Indian Airlines 2 hours and 5 minutes to Calcutta. On the plane there were 4 French poodles, and I ended up holding one of the poodles for most of the flight. Calcutta is a city of contrasts, where there is fabulous wealth and unbelievable poverty. We checked in to the Oberon Grand Hotel which is very much like a maze. Our guide took us shopping. Then later we had dinner at the hotel in the Prince's Nightclub. We were treated to Shish Kebab, cream of tomato soup, and a surprise soufflé.

July 8. The next morning it was sightseeing of Calcutta. We toured the Botanical Gardens, which have the world's largest Banyon tree, then the Palm House, and the Jain Hindu Temple. There we found cow dung baking on the walls which would later be used for fuel. Then we went to the Queen Victoria Memorial. There was a man in front of the memorial with 2 monkeys and a mongoose. We also saw many people relieving themselves in the trenches, and people were bathing in the streets. Others were getting a shave and haircut or just sleeping outside. At this time India has 550 million people. Lunch was at Prince's where we were served châteaubriand, vichyssoise, and pear belle Hélène. Our afternoon was free, but in the evening we left the hotel to see "Glimpses of India", a program which included Indian dancing plus several women modeling sarees. Dinner was at the Prince's Nightclub again.

July 9. The following morning we had another early flight. We got up at 4:30 and had breakfast served in our room. We left the hotel at 5:30 for an Indian Airlines 7:30 flight to Kathmandu, Nepal. Nepal is the land of the Gurka and the birthplace of Buddha. Lunch was at the Annapurna. Then there was sightseeing. We visited a Buddist temple, which reeked of urine. The Shirpers here are mountain people. We saw a stupa which is a kind of Buddhist shrine. The Parsees are a branch of Hinduism. They have a tower of Silence where a dead body is placed on the tower and the vultures take over. We saw monkeys at the Buddhist Temple. Then we went to the National Museum, then to the ancient city of Patan, which was built in 299. We visited the Golden Temple, then the ancient king's palace. Later we returned to the hotel where we saw movies on Nepal before dinner. The movies were supplied courtesy of Air France. In addition there was a black and white film on the Nepalese King's visit to Paris.

July 10. The next morning we left the Hotel de l'Annapurna at 7:30 A.M. It had rained all night and the right half of the only bridge crossing the river was partly washed away. That meant that we had to change from taxis to a bus in order to get through the 3 feet of water covering the bridge. The entire luggage was placed below on the bus, and it got really wet. Finally we got to the airport, but our plane couldn't land due to a 50-foot visibility level. So we were stranded at the airport for 6 hours not knowing if another plane would come for us. In the meantime, part of the bridge collapsed trapping us at the airport. The airline offered to feed us, but the kitchen was so dirty that I thought it best not to eat. Finally the plane arrived, and we got to fly to the holy Hindu city of Banaras. Dinner at the Clark's Hotel was consumée and lamb with rice.

July 11. The following morning we all got up early at 4:30 A.M. to make up for the sightseeing that we miss the day before. We took a boat ride on the Ganges. In order to reach the boat we had to walk through rows of lepers begging. We boarded the boat at one of the oldest bathing spots—2,000 years old. This was not a joyful boat ride. We passed some bloated bodies of babies floating in the river. If babies have not been baptized in the faith, they can't undergo cremation, which is the last of the Hindu rites. Cremation is to stop the cycle of reincarnation. The old and the sick go to Banaras to die. We passed the burning ghats where the bodies were clad in red cloth either burning or waiting to be burned. Cremation takes 3 hours and costs only the price of the wood. ($6.00 or $7.00) Also there are walls with niches where the old and the sick lie down to die. We returned to the hotel for lunch, but after the morning sightseeing, I wasn't very hungry.

In the afternoon we left the Clark's Hotel and visited the Monkey Temple where one of the monkeys bit one of our tour members on the leg while she was walking through the temple. Then we visited a festival, toured the university, then to a bazaar. We also visited a silk factory where they used real gold thread to make the Indian silk. Later we returned to the hotel for a 2-hour rest before leaving at 5:30 for the airport. This time we had a flight to Agra. This plane was also one hour late. In Agra we checked into the Clark's Shiraz Hotel

There are 4 castes in Hinduism: priest, warrior, businessman, and servant. Marriage is within the caste. A priest is devoted to humanity and is born a priest. He may marry and have children. Monks are not born a monk, and they are interested in self-improvement.

July 12. The next morning after breakfast, we took a long drive by taxi to Fatehpur Skirl, a city of red sandstone, built by the grandfather of the man who built the Taj Mahal, a man named Akbar. The city is a combination of Hindi and Moslem Architecture. After lunch we visited Agra, the city of sorrow and symbol of beauty. There we saw the Red Fort built in 1565 also by Åkbar. Then we drove to the Taj Mahal, which was built by Shah Jahan for his 3rd wife Mumtaz Mahal who died while giving birth to their 14th child. It was begun in 1631 and completed in 1648. It took 20,000 workmen employed daily to complete it. The Taj sits on the Jumna River, which has its beginnings in the Himalayas. At present both Shah Jahan and Mumtaz Mahal are entombed there. According to our guide, Shah Jahan could see the Taj being built while he was imprisoned in the Red Fort, but I could not find out why he was in prison. According to Wikipedia Emperor Shah Jahan described the Taj thusly: (Photo #28)

Photo #28

"Should guilty seek asylum here,
Like one pardoned, he becomes free from sin.
Should a sinner make his way to this mansion,
All his past sins are to be washed away.
The sight of this mansion creates sorrowing sighs;
And the sun and the moon shed tears from their eyes.
In this world this edifice has been made;
To display thereby the creator's glory."

Before leaving this beautiful white marble mausoleum, we had a group picture made in front as a beautiful souvenir. After the Taj visit, we stopped at a marble factory where they made plates and ashtray designs. I bought two mini plates with inlaid marble.

July 13. Most of the next day was at leisure, but in the evening we had a 25-minute flight to Delhi. En route to the airport, we stopped once more to bid adieu to the Taj Mahal. Our plane flight was at 16,000 feet. When we landed, we immediately checked into the Oberoi Intercontinental Hotel. Our dinner that evening finished at midnight, but it was delicious—pepper steak, baked potato, and carrots. We were to have 3 days here so part of our time was at leisure.

July 14. We did go sightseeing early the next morning to see New Delhi which is quite a modern city. We saw the tomb which set the example for the Taj Mahal, the Qutab Minar 230 foot Tower, the War Memorial, the American Embassy where Chester Bowles was the ambassador, and the Birla Temple, a temple which welcomes everyone, even the untouchables. Birla was the richest man in India. In addition he built the University Temple at the University of Banaras. We stopped at the Northland International where I bought a beautiful brass wine set. As usual we returned to the hotel for lunch.

Afterwards we left for sightseeing of Old Delhi and the Red Fort, a 17th century fort complex constructed by the Mughal emperor, Shah Jahan in the walled city. The fort is built on the Yamuna River, which fed the moats that surround many of the walls. Our most important stop that day was to the Raj Ghat, a memorial also on the Yamuna River, where Mahatma Gandhi was cremated. It is a black marble platform, and it marks the spot of Mahatma Gandhi's cremation on January 31, 1948, a day after his assignation. It is an impressive open memorial with an eternal flame at one end. Removal of shoes was necessary before approaching the Ghat as a show of respect. That evening we had Lobster Newburg for dinner along with rice and a baked potato.

July 15. Our entire day was at leisure. There were activities that we could attend: visitation of a school or private homes. I was too tired to do any of that. However there was a marriage going on at the hotel, and Mrs. Gandhi was due to arrive there soon.

Somewhere while traveling in the Far East, I had contracted amebic dysentery, and I could not shake it. I thought that I was being very careful. I did not drink the water, but I had a thermos that I used to carry water in order to moisten my face. Our faces were constantly being bombarded by dust. Also I had a washcloth that I carried with me and from time to time I would wet the washcloth using tap water from the thermos to cool my face. Then perhaps a day later I would pour bottled water into the thermos for drinking purposes. I never thought about the idea that dysentery germs might still be left in the thermos from the tap water. Anyway, I think that's how I got amebic dysentery.

From this point of my trip until the end, I proceeded to get weaker and weaker, and thinner and thinner. As to why I didn't come home, the answer is that I was too weak to come home alone. The thought of working my way back from half way around the world would take more strength than I had. It was far easier to stay with the group than to attempt a solo flight. I did see doctors frequently. They would come to the hotel, but they could not correctly diagnose my illness. They kept giving me vitamin shots in hopes of solving the problem. At the end of the trip, when I was back home, I went to my doctor who sent me immediately to the hospital. Yes, I did have amebic dysentery, and when given the correct medicine, I was back on the road to recovery within several days. Now back to the trip.

July 16. We left the hotel for a flight via Indian Airlines to Srinagar, India's most fashionable resort. We left Delhi at 9:30 A.M. and arrived at 11:30 A.M. Upon arrival a small boat called The *Honeymoon* picked us up and took us to our houseboat—*The Triumph*. (Photo #29) This picture of the *Triumph* was copied from the August 14, 1964, issue of *Life Magazine*.[1]

---

[1]   Life magazine, August 14, 1964, pp. 94-99

Photo #29

This is the Vale of Kashmir, a beautiful resort on the Dal River. We would stay on our houseboat for the next 3 days. Our boat had two bedrooms, a kitchen, and a living room plus attentive servants. Every morning upon waking, we would find a merchant in the living room with his wares spread out on the living room floor. Instead of us going to the market to shop, the market came to us. The first vendor had beautiful Indian Jewelry. When he left a second merchant arrived selling hats decorated with Snow Weasels, part of the ermine family. When he left a flower merchant arrived.

The *Triumph* must have been a popular boat because it also was pictured in *National Geographic Magazine*[2]

Water skiing and swimming and lots of ducks were all around us. During our stay we visited the beautiful Shalimar or Mogul Gardens built in the 1600's, then to the Nishat Gardens, then to the Kashmir Gardens also built by the Moguls. Our launch, the *Honeymoon*, took us for the garden visits.

July 17. The following day we visited a Papier Maché Factory then more Kashmir gardens. Then we returned to the *Triumph*. Later we went to a nearby houseboat, the *Zeffer*, for a farewell party for two of our participants. The food on our houseboat is somewhat lacking to my taste.

July 18. The next morning at 9:45 A.M. we all got into the *Honeymoon* for our next destination: Srinagar. We caught another Indian Airlines plane that took us to Amritsar in northern India. Then we got into private cars and crossed into Pakistan. Our lunch was at a private house near the border. There were very strict border formalities. Our ride from Amritsar to Lahore was 156 miles of dust. We had a cooler of soft drinks with us to help us cool off. Finally we reached our destination: Lahore, Pakistan. This city claims to have the largest mosque in the world, and according to Wikipedia it was until 1986 when other larger mosques began building. Now Wikipedia says it is the 5th largest mosque in the world. Our hotel, the Oberoi Faletti's Hotel, is just a mediocre hotel and our dinner followed suite.

---

[2]   National Geographic Magazine, November, 1958, pp. 610-611

July 19. The next morning we got up at 4:15 A.M. and had breakfast in our room. At 6:00 A.M. we were on Pakistan International Airways (PIA) for a flight to Peshawar, Pakistan. Our flight took 1-1/2 hours with one stop at Rawalpindi. Peshawar is known as the gateway of Central Asia. Its history is mixed with the writings of Kipling and the great conquerors of the past. The streets are filled with Uzbeks, Tajeks, Afridis, Shinwaris and Afghans. Bargaining is a way of life here. We checked into the Oberoi Dean's Hotel then set off for a 3-hour tour through the Kyber Pass to the Afghan border. Our small group was put into private cars. This is all just a tribal area with no police. Every man carries his own rifle. The village huts have openings for guns. The Moslem women are all dressed in black with their faces covered. This is the Pathan area all around Peshawar. According to Wikipedia, the oral tradition of Pathans is that they are descendants of the soldiers of Alexander the Great.

The Pathans are fierce warriors with blue eyes. Later that afternoon we were treated to a Tonga Ride, just a horse pulling a wagon called a Tonga. During the ride we met two Jordanian boys who wanted us to post letters for them to their families who are in the occupied area of Jordan. After dinner our guide gave us a Sitar Concert. The sitar is very like a guitar.

July 20. Early the next morning our group left the hotel in 3 taxis for the Kingdom of Swat. In order to do this we took the Malakand Pass thru the Malakand Mountains. En route we passed an army truck that was overturned because part of the road had given away. The ride to Swat was 110 miles, 40 of which were through the Malakand Pass. We reached

71

the summit of the Malakand Pass in the small city of Landi Kotal and visited the colorful market.

Rawalpindi is presently the capital of Pakistan. A new capital, Islamabad, is being built. Abdul Quadir Serhai, called the father of tourism in Pakistan, is our guide. The Kingdom of Swat is 4,000 square miles and is inhabited by Pathans. Swat is also the cradle of Buddhism. It is a small principality under the control of Pakistan. Our ride to Swat took us 4 hours. We met with the founder-king of Swat who is 82 years old. He greeted each one of us with a handshake. (Photo #30) He recited the beginning of the Koran to us and gave us an orange drink. Then he had his dancing monkey perform for us. Dinner at the Swat Hotel was really good. In the evening our guide talked to us about Kashmir and Pakistan. Our stay at the Swat Hotel is in the capital city of Saidu Sharif.

Photo #30

July 21. The next morning after breakfast at the Swat Hotel we left for a 40-mile tour of Swat Valley. We stopped for photos of Mankial Mountains, part of the Karakoram Range. After lunch we had a museum tour and visited some ancient Buddhist ruins.

July 22. The next morning we left Swat for a 4-hour ride to Peshawar. We were in the same hotel, but this time we had a better room. Our room has limited water usage, only 3 hours in the morning and 4 hours at night. In the afternoon the guide and I took a Tonga ride around Peshawar.

July 23. The following morning we left the hotel at 9:00 A.M. for the airport. We have a special flight on Ariana Afghan Airlines. It was a short flight, only lasting 1 hour, but it was interesting. We flew over the mountains and Khyber Pass, then landing in Kabul, Afghanistan. Our room was at the Kabul Hotel, which had no air-conditioning and no fans. We did, however, have a nice lunch before we began our sightseeing of Kabul. Workers in Kabul can have their lunch delivered topside.

(Photo #31)

According to our guidebook Kabul is a photographer's delight and is seldom visited by tourists. It is a city never-to-be-forgotten with its colorful bazaars and hand woven fabrics, carved trinkets, and valuable coins, not to mention the tribal nomads as they pass through with their camel caravans. Afghanistan is primarily Muslim. We drove through the city stopping at a museum before visiting the tomb of the former king who was assassinated in 1933 by a college student. His son is the present ruler. We visited the old city. We drove down to the entrance of the Kyber Pass but did not cross over. Afghanistan was still in the middle of a dust storm and dust was everywhere.

July 24. The next morning after breakfast we left for the city of Istalif, which is 25 miles away and famous for its blue pottery; however the pottery is very primitive according to our standards. Nevertheless, I bought a small dish for a souvenir. Then we returned to the hotel for lunch, which was large in my opinion. Since the weather was so hot and dusty, our tourist agency decided to treat us to dinner at a special restaurant called Nazars where we had two kinds of rice dishes, salad, spinach, kebabs, vegetable soup, melon and veal—a typical Afghani dinner.

July 25. At 7:00 A.M. the next morning after breakfast, we left the hotel for a flight from Kabul to Teheran, stopping only once at Kandahar for 45 minutes. American money built this airport, but planes only stop 3 times a week here. What a waste of our money! On the flight I sat beside an Afghani man who was a flight engineer for Ariana Afghan Airlines. He bought me a Danish beer, and told me that his salary was $55.00 a month. He also said that passports were very hard to get in Afghanistan, and they are only good for one year. After landing we checked into the Royal Teheran Hilton Hotel where we are staying. I was too sick to eat dinner.

July 26. Early the following morning we left the hotel at 6:15 A.M. for an Iran Airlines flight at 7:30 A.M. Those were the days when it was really enjoyable to travel—no need to get to the airport early, no security lines, just plain travel. Our flight to Isfahan took 1 hour 10 minutes. Upon arrival we checked into the Shah Abbas Hotel, then left for sightseeing right away. We saw the Palace of the Forty Pillars. Actually there were only 20 pillars, but their reflection in the nearby pool made them look like there were 40 pillars. It was built by Shah Abbas the Great. Then we visited the Shah's Mosque-Masjid-E-Shah which also was built by Shah Abbas. Afterwards, we returned to the hotel for a large lunch, then more sightseeing in the afternoon. We saw the Sheikh

Lutfollah Mosque built by Shah Abbas as a ladies mosque with a private tunnel. Afterwards our group was treated to a visit to a rug factory. Then we were off to a bazaar where a camel was grinding yellow turmeric, and men were making wood blocks and stamping prints. They also were dying prints. We also visited the Emami Miniature Factory where I bought two miniatures painted on camel bone. Almost all of my souvenirs have been given away or lost, but these two unique miniatures are still on my bedroom walls. Following was a visit to a 2,000-year-old fire temple which was still standing. Then we were off to Menar Jonban, the shaking minarets. We passed over the Khaju Bridge with 33 arches like the Ponte Vecchio in Florence. We returned to the hotel for dinner. Afterwards we were served tea in the Turkish garden.

July 27. The next day we left the Shah Abbas Hotel for a 55-minute flight to Shiraz, the city of roses and nightingales. Upon arrival we drove immediately to Persepolis, a distance of 40 miles, to visit the tombs of Xerxes, Darius the Great, Darius II, and Artaxerxes I. After lunch we had one hour of rest before we visited the city of Persepolis which was built by Darius in 515 B.C. for festivals. In 331 B.C. Alexander the Great burned it. Later the Arabs defaced the bas-reliefs. In the background are tombs of Artaxerxes II and III. There is a famous tablet usually in the museum at Teheran, and later at Expo Montreal, Quebec, Canada, which gives the names of the workers at Persepolis thus proving that it was not built by slave labor like the pyramids. We spent 1-1/2 hours working through the ruins at Persepolis in the beating sun. Then we returned to Shiraz where we visited the tombs of two major

Iranian poets—Sa'adi and Hafiz. The Iranians really like both poets. This was a big sightseeing day, and we still had a return flight to Isfahan, and back to Teheran. The first flight was really scary. It was dusk, and we were landing near the mountains, and the radar was not working. Then we still had our flight to Teheran. We were really glad to get to Teheran and dinner.

July 28. The next morning we had sightseeing of Teheran and lots of time to visit the interesting bazaars. The afternoon included the Golestan Palace, the archeological and fine arts museums and the world's most spectacular crown jewels.

July 29. We left the hotel and drove to Qazvin. We stopped at an old mosque and private home. Then we were off to a 125-mile ride to Hamadan. We arrived at 3:00 P.M. and had lunch at Bou'Ali Hotel. Later we visited the tomb of a Muslim philosopher, Avincenna, then the tomb of Esther and cousin Mordecai. We visited another carpet factory and drove outside the city to see ancient Iran. After dinner at the hotel, we spent the night at Hamadan.

July 30. After breakfast the next morning we left the hotel for a 3-1/2 hour ride to Kermanshah. En route we saw a bas-relief of Cyrus dating from 529 B.C. We also stopped at the Taq-e Bostan Grotto for another bas-relief. Lunch was at the hotel in Kermanshah. Later we drove through the city before returning to Hamadan for dinner.

July 31. The following morning we left the Bou Ali Hotel at 6:15 A.M. for a long ride back to Teheran. En route we stopped in Qazvin to see the not-too-interesting Shah Mosque. We arrived at the Teheran Hilton in time for lunch.

Then we had time to clean up and relax before the hotel dinner.

August 1. The next morning we left the hotel in 3 cars. This was not a good day for us. One of our tour members got sick. One of our cars broke down, and we had to wait while it was being repaired. When the car repair was finished, we continued our trip to Chalus where we would stay at Hotel Tchalous. Now we are dragging our feet. We left home June 9, towards the end of the Six-Day War, and we were en route not knowing how the war might affect our itinerary. What we really had to do was drag our feet in Iran. So we got to see a lot more of Iran than expected. Our planned visits to Lebanon, Syria, Egypt, Jordan, and Israel were compromised, and instead we would see all the back roads of Iran and Turkey due to the Six-Day War. So from July 27 until August 12, we were rerouted due to the Six Day War.

August 2. Next we left the hotel after breakfast for Pahlavi. En route we visited a tea factory. After lunch we visited a caviar factory. Then we drove to the Caspian Sea for a 2-hour swim, and then 4 hours back to the Ramsar Hotel. We are certainly seeing much more of Iran than was shown in the itinerary. We were supposed to stay in the Ramsar Hotel, but we couldn't due to a summit meeting of Iran, Pakistan, and Turkey. So we drove back to Chalus.

August 3. The next morning after breakfast we left the hotel at 7:30 A.M. and drove to Teheran via a scenic route. We arrived at the Royal Teheran Hilton at 1:30. We had the rest of the afternoon at leisure in Teheran.

August 4. We left the hotel early at 4:30 A.M. for a 6:30 Pan American flight #001 to Istanbul. Our plane did stop in Beirut after a 2-1/2 hour flight. Then our plane continued to Istanbul. We had an afternoon rest at the Istanbul Hilton; then we visited the local bazaars. In the evening after dinner, we had a long drive along the Bosporus.

August 5. The next day we had a lot of free time, but we did get to visit the famous St. Sophia. (Hagia Sophia) Our hotel, the Istanbul Hilton, was situated overlooking the entrance to the Black Sea and we could watch the Russian boats coming from Egypt.

August 6. This was a completely free day to explore as we wished.

August 7. We left the hotel and took a 10-minute ferry ride across the Bosporus to Scutari—a place in Asia where Florence Nightingale nursed during the Crimean War. We then drove 1/2 hour and crossed the Sea of Marmara from north to south. We got on a boat at Kartal. The Dardanelles connect the Sea of Marmara and the Aegean. The Bosporus connects the Black Sea to the Sea of Marmara. Later in the day we visited the tomb of Osman Gazi, the first Turkish Sultan. The tomb is near the Acropolis. There was also a visit to the tomb of the Sultan Murat II. We visited the home of Sultan Murat. The Moslums don't decorate the mosques with pictures or statues. Hence they use picture writing in their homes. The Plane Tree is to Teheran as the Sycamore Tree is to Istanbul. Then we toured the Green Mausoleum of Sultan Mehmet, and then to the Green Mosque and bazaar, then back to the hotel for dinner.

August 8. We stayed in Çanakkale, Hotel Trova. In the morning we drove to Bandirna for lunch. Then we returned to Çanakkale. It's a terrible hotel, but the view is good. We are right on the Dardanelles.

August 9. We left the hotel and drove 30 km to Troy where we had a one-hour visit of the ancient city. This is the city of Homer's <u>Iliad</u>. Then we drove to Ayvalik for lunch. Ayvalik, a small seaside town, is right on the Aegean coast. Then we drove to Pergamum to view the ruins of the Acropolis. According to the book of Revelation, Pergamum is where Satan had his throne. Our next stop was Izmir where we checked in at the Buyuk Efes Hotel, one of the oldest hotels in Izmir just one block from the beach.

August 10. After breakfast we left for Ephesus where we visited St. John's Basilica and the Tomb and the Temple of Artemis. We walked the marble Arcadian Way and visited the Virgin Mary's house where she lived after Jesus's death. She may have died there although she may be buried in Jerusalem. We had lunch near Mary's home then returned to Izmir where we drove around the city.

August 11. The following morning we got up very early and caught Flight #208 on Turkish Airlines to Ankara. The flight lasted 1 hour 45 minutes. Once on the ground we drove 25 km. to the Grand Hotel in Ankara. Our room was very small but nice. After lunch at the hotel we left for a city sightseeing tour. We visited the Hittite Museum which was very modern and well planned. Then we drove to the Temple of Augustus next to the Haci Bayram Mosque, the largest mosque in Ankara. Then we toured the Roman Baths, then to Ataturk's Tomb and Mausoleum.

August 12. The following morning we left Ankara on Turkish Airlines Charter by Air France and landed in Istanbul. We checked in to the Istanbul Hilton Hotel where we had lunch. In the afternoon we visited the many bazaars, then rode up the Bosporus for a view of Galata Tower and the Castle of Mohamet the Conqueror. When we returned to the city, we had a visit of the Blue mosque, which is a mixture of the Ottoman and Byzantine architecture. The mosque is unique with its six minarets. Dinner was at the Hilton Skylight Room.

August 13. After breakfast we headed to the airport for an Air France flight to Athens. On the flight a gentleman who sat next to me gave me 15 drachmas (about 50 cents) because he told me that I would need that amount to handle my luggage upon arrival. The flight lasted one hour and 10 minutes, and Air France provided free bus service to the terminal. Our city sightseeing tour included the Temple of Dionysius, the Acropolis, the Olympic Stadium, the Royal Palace, the Temple of Olympian Zeus, and Hadrian's Arch. That evening our group went to a Sound and Light Program which included Greek folk dancing. It was held at the Parthenon. We were staying at the Athens Hilton Hotel.

August 14. We had a restful morning and then left the hotel in the afternoon to visit a government store with fixed prices. I bought a lot of souvenirs at this store-a gold Parthenon charm for my charm bracelet, some yellow worry beads, and some small jewelry items. We then drove to Sounion to visit the Temple of Poseidon (Neptune) by the sea. It was built in the 5th century B.C. just like the Parthenon. The view from Cape Sounion looking out to the

Aegean Sea was fantastic. Then we all had a coffee/coke break on the beach overlooking the Aegean. It was good to relax and mentally review all the places that we had visited on this Round the World Trip. We saw so many unique things and places. Afterwards we returned to the Hilton for dinner.

August 15. We left the hotel at 8:00 A.M. after breakfast and drove to the Gulf of Corinth. A canal connects the Ionian Sea on the right and the Aegean Sea on the left. Then we drove to Argos and then to Epidaurus to visit the amphitheatre, which is famous for its acoustics. We stopped at Nauphlia for lunch at the Amphitryo Hotel. Later we drove to Mycenae to see the tomb of the Mycenaean king Agamemnon and the Lion Gate, which is nothing more than two headless lions separated by a symbolic pillar. The German archeologist, Heinrich Schliemann, supposedly discovered the Lion Gate Monument.

Agamemnon was the leader of the Greeks who attacked the city of Troy during the Trojan War. Later we drove back to Corinth to visit the Temple of Apollo. Afterwards we returned to the Hilton Hotel for dinner in the Ta Nissia Restaurant. At dinner I tried my hands at escargot. We also had tournedos, then chocolate ice cream, and Cointreau. Afterwards we went to the Roof Garden Bar to view the Parthenon illuminated at night along with St. George's Monastery. The illumination stops at 11:30 P.M. when they turn the lights off. One of the tour members bought me a bourbon and coke to celebrate my birthday which was the following day.

August 16. I celebrated my 35th birthday on a one-day cruise to Hydra, a small island in the Aegean Sea. Later when we returned, we all had our farewell dinner at the Tavern Kalokerines. Our Travcoa guide, Dave, bought all the women gardenias. We enjoyed a typical Greek dinner: meat pâté wrapped in grape leaves, local wine with resin, and veal roast. The orchestra played Happy Birthday to me, and we all had a piece of birthday cake. Our restaurant is right by the Parthenon with a super view. We ate in the open on the roof. Since this was our last night together, we all stayed up late and didn't return to the hotel until 1:00 A.M.

August 17. We got up at 8:30 A.M. and weighed our luggage. Mine weighed 21 kilos. At 10:15 we left for the airport for the TWA Flight home. Our flight was non-stop. When we got to the end of the runway, the plane returned to the hangar due to a faulty rudder. However, this was only a 1-hour delay. There is a 6-hour time difference between New York and Athens. Our flight took 10 hours to reach New York. Our plane was a 707, and we had lots of legroom. We were scheduled to refuel at Gander, Newfoundland, but it was unnecessary. What a great trip, and this would be followed by many more great trips. There was one downside, however, for this trip. I arrived home very weak from the amebic dysentery and had to be treated at the hospital. Such is one of the dangers of world travel.

Note: Today I would like to thank the B.O.A.C. baggage handlers in Ceylon who stole my two cartons of Viceroys while my luggage was in storage. Although I was really irritated at the time, it made me realize what a deadly monkey I had on my back. In 1967 I had little knowledge about the damaging power of cigarettes. That September, I gave up cigarettes for good. Now I have been nicotine-free for 45+ years.

Chapter Seven

1968 Travcoa 69 Day African Safari Tour

Since I had the travel bug, I was always planning my next trip while still on my current trip. So my next choice would be another trip with Travcoa, this time in Africa on a picture safari for 69 days. My plane tickets included the following flights: Cincinnati, New york, Dakar, Bamako, Timbuktu, Bamako, Abidjan, Accra, Johannesburg, Durban, Lourenco Marques, Johannesburg, Bulawayo, Victoria Falls, Wankie, Salisbury, Blantyre, Dar es Salaam, Zanzibar, Mombasa, Moshi, Nairobi, Entebbe, Nairobi, Addis Ababa, Asmara, Khartoum, Cairo, Paris, New York, Cincinnati, for a total of 30 flights. The land portion of this trip was $2350.00. The entire airfare from New York and return was $1140.00. So the total price of this trip is just about $3500.00 for Deluxe and First Class Hotels, 3 meals a day, sightseeing including entrance fees and guides, transportation of 2 normal Pullman suitcases, all gratuities to hotel staff and guides plus the services of a tour manager. The tour did not include our passport, visas, or tourist cards.

June 17. 1968, my friend, Clarence, drove me to the American Airlines Terminal in Cincinnati for an 11:45 A.M. flight #240 to New York Kennedy Airport. When we landed I had to find the Air Afrique Airlines which was part of the

Pan American System. Air Afrique offered 2 weekly flights to Africa. At the airport I met Tony James, our Travcoa guide, who would accompany us for the next 69 days. Our flight RK#022 to Dakar was scheduled to leave at 7:00 P.M., but we were delayed an hour waiting for ground clearance. The flight lasted 7 hours. Alcoholic drinks were 50 cents. Dinner included stuffed guinea hen. We landed about 8:00 A.M. in Dakar and were driven to our hotel, the N'Gor Hotel. We had a good view, but the room was mediocre.

June 18. We got to sleep late since we were sleep deprived after the flight from New York. After lunch we visited the colorful village markets, then drove to Soumbedioune Village and Corniche. We also visited the Great Mosque at Dakar plus the fishing village of Cayar.

June 19. The next morning after breakfast we left in a boat for Gorée Island. The trip lasted ½ hour each way. Gorée Island used to be the center of the slave trade. We visited the old slave quarters and then the market place. We had lunch on the island. Then we returned to Dakar and visited the cathedral. Dinner was at the hotel. Our flight to Bamako for the following day had to be postponed one day since the plane was too small for all 16 of us.

June 20. After breakfast we left for M'Bour where we had lunch. Then we journeyed to Joal, which was 75 miles from Dakar. From there we crossed a causeway to Fadiouth, a village built on a shell island. We returned by pirogue, a native canoe made of a hollowed tree trunk. Our return was via Rufisque. Dinner that evening was at 7:30 in a shack hut near the ocean.

June 21. After a light breakfast, we left on a charter flight via Air Senegal, a 4-hour flight from Dakar to Bamako. Upon arrival we had lunch at Le Motel. At 4:00 P.M. We left for sightseeing. We crossed the Niger River to visit the stadium, the swimming pool, and the university. This was not an interesting day, and it was not enhanced by the morning flight, which was terrible.

June 22. We got up at 4:00 A.M. for a 6:00 A.M. three-legged flight to Timbuktu, Mali, via Mopti and Goundam. This was a memorable and unusual flight. We were on an old paratrooper plane left over from the war. Since the plane was used by soldiers, there was no private restroom on the plane just a toilet situated in the middle/back of the plane. When I saw that, I decided there was no way I would entertain the idea of using the facilities.

The city of Timbuktu has several different spellings of its name as well as many different versions about how it got its name. For us in America, it means some unknown area at the end of the world. Timbuktu is on the southern edge of the Sahara Desert north of the Niger River. Camel caravans still come to the market place, and the slave market continues. Veiled Taureg men walk the streets. French is the official language in Mali.

The Timbuktu Hotel is terrible by our standards. This place really is the end of the earth. It is like the original Caravancerie with one ceiling light and a marginal bathroom. The hotel had no dining room, but a table was set up in the hotel lobby right in front of the check-in desk, and this was where we had dinner. There was no air-conditioning and no screens. Our beds had no mosquito netting to cover us. The temperature seemed to be 120 F. I skipped lunch since it was too hot to eat.

Our rooms were not in the hotel proper, but they were in separate buildings in back of the hotel. At night there was no lighting leading to our rooms so we had to use our hands and follow the outside wall by feeing our way along the wall. The problem with this tactic was that the wall was the favorite abode of salamanders so we had to be careful where we put our hands. Our toilet in our room was unique. The toilet seat was a cut-out piece of cardboard. (Photo #32)

Photo #32

At 4:00 P.M. we started our tour of this famous city. First there was a mosque and the market. Then we visited the house of Major Alexander Gordon Laing, the first white man to reach Timbuktu. We saw the local oven where they baked

88

their bread along with the Taureq Tribesman. Taureq Knives are a speciality of Timbuktu.

We saw several camel caravans, and noticed that the women were all veiled. We then drove 4 km. to the Niger River Harbor, then returned to the hotel. My tour members wanted me to telephone our tour company to find out how soon we could get out of this place. Since the language spoken in this region was French, I was chosen to communicate with the tourist office. I asked them to expedite our departure since we wanted to leave this place, the sooner, the better.

Later at 8:00 we had dinner in the hotel lobby. A dance started at 9:00 P.M. and lasted until 1:30 A.M. This was a welcome diversion since it was too hot to sleep anyway. Charlie, one of our tour participants, located his flashlight so he used it to lead us back to our rooms. Once we got to our rooms, we were really trapped inside since going outside was just stumbling around in the dark. I slept about 1-1/2 hours.

June 23. We got up at 5:00 A.M. and left the hotel right after breakfast. The plane left at 8:00 A.M., and we returned the same way; however our return trip was about 20 minutes faster. The flight made me sick due to the high altitude.

We returned to the same hotel that we had when we arrived in Mali. Lunch at the hotel was fish and mangoes. In the afternoon we took a long bus ride to the President's Palace, the Arts & Crafts Workshop, and the Niger River Rapids. I was too sick to eat dinner. They sent a tomato salad and tea to my room, but I could not eat. I went to bed early.

June 24. We left Bamako at 8:00 A.M. after getting up at 4:00 A.M. I was too dizzy to carry my things so one of our participants carried my purse and cameras. We flew to the Ivory Coast city of Abidjan and checked in to the Ivoire Hotel. It is part of the Inter-Continental Chain and is a beautiful hotel. I went to the bowling alley for lunch. The others went on a city sightseeing tour. When I returned to the hotel, a nurse at the hotel gave me two pills and a vitamin shot which hurt an hour afterwards. Later I joined the group for a nice dinner in the main dining room of the hotel.

June 25. The next morning I felt much better so after breakfast we left the hotel at 9:00 for an all-day tour. We drove to Bingerville, the second capital of the Ivory Coast, where we visited an orchid plantation and a craft shop, then to the Grand-Bassam, the first capital of the Ivory Coast. After lunch in Grand-Bassam, we returned to the hotel via a fishing village. That evening we had a great dinner at the Carioca Restaurant on the 12th floor of our hotel. The restaurant specialized in Brazilian food. The panorama of the city was superb.

June 26. We got up at 9:00 A.M. and had a late breakfast at the hotel. We sat around the hotel lobby until 11:00; then we left for the airport. I left $2.00 in an envelop for the nurse. We had lunch at the airport, and we left at 1:30 P.M. on an Air Afrique jet to Accra, Ghana. It was a wonderful flight that lasted only 50 minutes. We checked into the Ambassador Hotel where we had a second lunch. The hotel is an Inter-Continental Hotel but is in poor shape. The afternoon was at leisure. Later we had dinner at the hotel.

June 27. After breakfast, we left the hotel at 9:00 for morning sightseeing of Accra including the National Museum, the Parliament Buildings, the University of Ghana, Christiansborg Castle, Independence Arch, and the Black Star Arch. At the market place I bough two Ashanti dolls for $2.00 each. The roommate that I had on last year's trip had advised me that Ghana would be the place to buy the Ashanti Fertility Dolls, and it would be a worthwhile purchase if I could find them. If seems that Ghana is the only place to buy them. Then later I bought 2 more for $1.50 each. All the tour participants were surprised that I had bought the native dolls, and they felt that I had wasted my money. Later we had lunch at the Ambassador Hotel. The afternoon was free for letter writing and leisure. Dinner again was at the hotel. We were advised to go straight to bed since we had to get up at 1:15 A.M. for our next adventure. We left the hotel at 2:15, and our Boeing 707 plane left at 3:30 A.M. for Johannesburg. The flight lasted 5-1/2 hours, and there was a 2-hour time change. Before landing we were served breakfast on board.

June 28. We checked in at the Rand International Hotel in Johannesburg, South Africa. We had lunch at the hotel and time afterwards for a nap before dinner. My new roommate had not yet arrived. My former roommate left the trip in Accra since she had only booked a partial trip. This is not summer here, but winter. My room is cold. The outside temperature is between 35 and 40 degrees.

June 29. Breakfast as usual was at the Rand Hotel, then city sightseeing of Johannesburg. We visited a gold mine and the Albert Hertzog Tower. We returned to the hotel for lunch. We had free time in the afternoon before dinner at the hotel. We then left for a Camelot film.

June 30. After breakfast we left at 9:00 for the mine dances in Pretoria about 35 miles outside the city. There were 8 dances, then an intermission. Then there were 6 more dances. The entire trip lasted about 2 hours. We returned to the hotel for lunch. Afterwards the group went to the museum. Later we all moved our luggage into one room in preparation for our next trip. We had a nice dinner at the hotel: rock lobster, peas and iced tea. We remained at the hotel until 9:00 P.M. when we left for the train to Kimberly where we shared compartments. I treated myself to a beer before retiring.

July 1. The porters woke us up at 6:45 A.M., and we had a light breakfast. We arrived at Kimberly at 8:00. First we went to see the German Shepherd Training School. The dogs are trained to guard the De Beers Diamond Mine. Then we went to the De Beers Diamond Mine where we had lunch at the Horseshoe Motel. Following lunch we went to the Big Hole surrounded by museums. (Photo #33) We visited the Duggan Cronin Museum where there were many photographs that Dugan had made of the various tribes. We visited a Zulu hut and a Tswana hut before visiting the Oppenheim Memorial Garden. Then we saw a native village. We returned to the Horseshoe Motel, picked up our luggage, and left immediately for the train station.

Photo #33

We caught the famous Blue Train to Cape Town at 6:25 P.M. During the night we had a three-hour delay due to a problem caused by another train on the same track. We spent the night on the Blue Train, appropriately named since all the cars were a royal blue, except for the two engines which were a bright red. The Blue Train covers the 999 miles between Pretoria and Cape Town and is the pride of the South African Railways. It has air-conditioned compartments, a beautiful dining room, a lounge, and an observation car. The furnishings are all a soft blue, and the staff of this luxury train is chosen to provide the best possible service.

July 2. We had breakfast and lunch on the Blue Train, and we arrived in Cape Town at 2:30 P.M. Upon arrival we went directly to Table Bay for our cable car ride to the top of Table Mountain. It rains a lot in Cape Town, and it is sometimes difficult to view the city of Cape Town and the surroundings in inclement weather. When we began the ride to the top, the weather was fine. When we reached the top, it was raining. Afterwards we checked into the Grand Hotel and then had dinner at the hotel. The weather was very cold and had reached a new all-time low.

July 3. After breakfast we left the hotel for a city sightseeing tour. We visited the Castle of Good Hope in the rain, and then went to the Natural History Museum. Lunch was back at the hotel. We went shopping in the afternoon. Dinner at the hotel was in celebration of one of the participant's birthday.

July 4. After breakfast we left for an all-day tour. Our first stop was for morning tea at Kommetjie Hotel. Then we traveled to Cape Point on the Cape of Good Hope. Lunch was at the New King's Hotel at Kalk Bay, a small fishing village near Cape Town. We had white and red wine at lunch to celebrate the 4th of July. Then we visited the Groot Constantia Wine Farm, the oldest and most historic wine farm in South Africa. We returned to the hotel for dinner in the Florentine Room.

July 5. We had the entire day at leisure. I spent a lot of time shopping for African jewelry and long underwear. I returned to the Constantia Room at the hotel for lunch. Later we all met for dinner in the Florentine room. The rest of the evening was spent packing for our 10-day garden tour which would begin the next day.

July 6. We left the hotel after breakfast, but stopped for morning tea at the Garden Route Hotel in Riviersonderend, a small town at the beginning of the Garden Route in South Africa. The town is located on the Sonderend River. Then we drove to the Albertinia Hotel for lunch. Afterwards we stopped at the Wilderness Hotel at Wilderness, a seaside town on the Garden Route of the southern Cape of South Africa. All during the morning and afternoon rides, we were treated to views of animals such as zebras, bondeboks, elands, and baboons. At night we returned to the Wilderness Hotel. Our room had a heater high on the wall that turned on with a chain. The hotel staff put a hot water bottle in our bed for our comfort. Also we had large feather comforters on our beds.

July 7. After breakfast we went to the Highgate Ostrich Farm for tea. We watched the ostriches race, and we got to have our picture taken while sitting on top of an ostrich. Later we returned to the Wilderness Hotel for lunch. Then we took a 2 hour 45 minute ride to Plettenberg Bay where we stayed at the Formosa Inn. The Inn is laid out like a motel with no heat in the cabins. We spent most of the time in the lodge where there was a fire in the fireplace. For sleeping there was another hot water bottle in our bed. I did have to buy a pair of men's underwear to wear under my slacks due to the winter in this part of the world. The underwear was also useful for sleeping.

July 8. After breakfast at the hotel we drove through the Tzittzikama Forest to Stormsrivier where we had tea at the Tzitzikama Forest Inn. They had all kinds of cookies for us. Then we drove to Port Elizabeth where we stayed at the Marine Hotel. Our lunch also was at the Marine Hotel. Later we went to the Snake Park where we caught the 3:00 P.M. show. Then we went next door for the Dolphin show at the Oceanarium. We also stopped and visited with the Xhosa

Tribe, the Pondo Tribe, the Tempo Tribe, and the Zulus. We returned to the Marine Hotel for dinner which was in the Skyroof Restaurant.

July 9. After breakfast at the hotel we left at 9:30 and drove through the Kaffir border country via the Cathedral City of Grahamstown. We stopped at the Graham Hotel in Grahamstown for lunch then drove to East London. Our first stop was the museum where we saw the huge Latimeria Chalumnae Fish, named in honor of Marjorie Courtenay-Latimer and the waters in which it was found. We also got to see the penguin pool on the Esplanade. Finally we drove to the Dean's Hotel where they had fruit in the room and a heater. Dinner was in the famous old dining room.

July 10. After breakfast we left for a morning drive through the Transkei which is all controlled by the Bantu. Morning tea was at the Butterworth Hotel. Then we drove through the Ciskei area, which is jointly controlled by the Xhosa tribesmen called the "Red Blanket" people. We ended up at Umtata for lunch at the Savoy Hotel. This is also where we spent the night. There was no heat in the hotel, but hot water bottles were available. After a meager lunch, we left with Mr. L.H. Hunter for a visit to a nearby Bantu Village—the Pondo Tribe where we saw the primitive customs of the girls cooking, making up, grinding corn and dancing.

Their enclosures are called kraals, and they are made out of 11x14 clay blocks, and then plastered with 3 parts of cow manure and 1 part earth. The women make the clay blocks, and the men assemble them. Then the women plaster. The roof goes on whole on stays. Women gather grass and the men thatch. There are no graveyards in this part of South

Africa. They are buried sometimes in blankets, sometimes in coffins, but there are no markers. Water is carried from miles around. There are no toilets, only nature that leaves no odor.

Their red blankets start out as white. Then red ochre is pounded into them. Only unmarried girls have bare breasts. The women wear copper and plastic jewelry which cuts into their arms and legs. They want their legs to have a stout appearance. Mr. Hunter paid the people for their dancing by poker chips which are later redeemable by money. En route we stopped at his curio shop where I bought some beaded necklaces and bracelets. We returned to the Savoy Hotel. At 6:00 P.M. Mr. Hunter showed us a film that he had made on circumcision. Later I went to bed with 2 hot water bottles and my long johns.

The film on circumcision was not a pleasant experience, but I will attempt to describe it. The men are circumcised from ages 17 to 21. The whole process lasts three months. It is partly psychological since it signals the entrance into manhood and the end of childish things. A hut is built for the boys—thatch only. The ceremony is performed by the witch doctor. The foreskin is severed with a knife. It would not have the psychological impact if it were done as a child. Once cut it is wrapped in onionskin, and then tied with goatskin cords. No anesthetic whatsoever is used and no modern equipment.

For seven days they stay alone with nothing to eat but unsalted corn and water with ashes. This is done to prevent heavy eating and drinking since urinating is very difficult especially if salt has been eaten. On the eighth day the dancing starts. Also the boys are given roasted corn, lamb from a slaughtered sheep, and homemade beer. The first mouthful of all three items must be spit out to prove their self-control. Their bodies are covered with clay and later with white ochre which is left on for three months until the Great Wash. After the Great Wash, bodies are smeared with animal fat and red ochre. No trace of white must remain. Boys cut the corn stalk looking for the corn bore worm. They bite off its head and squeeze the fluid around their operation because it acts as a soothing salve to ease the itching caused by the healing process. When the ceremony is finished, the hut is burned to the ground. The boy is given a red blanket, and he goes off to his family.

July 11. We left the Savoy Hotel after breakfast and drove to Mount Frère where we had tea and cakes at the Frontier Hotel. We continued our drive to the Royal Hotel in Kokstad for lunch. Afterwards we left the Cape Province area and crossed into Natal. For afternoon tea we stopped at the Plough Hotel in Ixopo. It was patterned after a British tearoom. Then we drove to Pietermaritzburg, the city of flowers, and on to our hotel, the Imperial. We had an early dinner due to a scheduled movie afterwards in Queen Elizabeth Park. It was a film on wildlife conservation. Since 1900 one animal per year has been made extinct.

July 12. We left the Imperial Hotel after breakfast for a city sightseeing tour of Pietermaritzburg. This city is the capital of Natal Province. We visited the Voortrekkers' Museum and the Church Of The Vow built when God helped the Voortrekkers revenge the brutal murder of Pier Retief and his 69-member party by Dingaan and the Zulu king. Dingaan had a treaty with Retief who promised to retrieve

Dingaan's stock which was stolen by some men. Retief kept his part of the bargain, but Dingaan murdered him. Retief's murder was revenged by a handful of Voortrekkers. This was considered a miracle and the Dutch Reform Church Of the Vow was built in 1840. Then we drove to Drummond to view the Valley of a Thousand Hills. This is the scenic attraction of this area. We also saw the Zulu Kraal and some Zulu Tribal dancing. A man and 3 of his 9 wives danced for us. The Zulus are polygamous. The man usually stays with his first wife. He asks permission of the lead wife to visit other wives and generally divides his time among them. I had my picture taken with the Zulu chief. (Photo #34) This was also our tea break for the afternoon.

Photo #34

It is 1500 miles from Durban to Cape Town along the Garden Route. We arrived at the Edward Hotel in Durban. Durban was founded by Vasgo de Gama in 1400. It is a large industrial port of about 600,000 and has a large Indian population, that was brought into the country for the sugar cane industry. My roommate and I have Room 207 that is right on the Indian Ocean with a balcony and heat. The hotel management sent us 3 red roses to decorate our room. Music plays in the bathroom. We had lunch in the Smorgasbord Restaurant. Afterwards we went shopping on

West Street for souvenirs. Dinner was at the hotel at the Causerie where they had dancing. Dinner was vichyssoise, Châteaubriand, and crepes Suzettes.

July 13. As usual we had breakfast at the hotel before beginning a city sightseeing tour. Our first stop was the Indian Market where I bought a copper plaque of giraffes. We then returned to the hotel for lunch, which was rock lobster, strawberries and ice cream. Our afternoon was at leisure so I bought a book, *Uhuru*, by Robert Ruark. Then I used my hotel card for a free drink. I got Pimm's No 2, a tall drink with slices of apple, cucumber, oranges and 2 cherries. It is made of gin or rum and bitter lemon. Dinner was in the Edward Restaurant.

July 14. We had breakfast on the hotel terrace. Durban is considered the playground of South Africa so it was very interesting to explore the city. After breakfast I went on a long walk with Tony, our Travcoa guide, and Charles, one of our fellow travelers. I'll write more about Charles later. Lunch was at the Smorgasbord Restaurant. At 2:30 we went to the Japanese Garden. Then we went to a place where they had Zulu dancing. Dinner was back at the hotel. Then later we took another walk.

July 15. This was a complete day at leisure so after breakfast I went shopping again. I bought some jewelry, and then I returned to the hotel for lunch. Charles and I took a ride in one of the Zulu Rickshaws. Later I telephoned Dana, the Indian who had sold me the hand-tooled copper plaque of giraffes. I was interested in purchasing more of the hand-tooled coppers so he brought 3 more designs to the hotel. I ended up buying 3 more of his hand-tooled copper plaques. These three cost me $80.00 and that included postage to the U.S. Today all 4 of these beautiful copper plaques are hanging high up on my great room wall, and they are a daily souvenir, a reminder of a fantastic trip. Dinner was in the Causerie where we had chilled consommé, filet mignon, strawberries and ice cream. Later we took a small walk after dinner.

July 16. As usual breakfast was at the hotel. At 8:00 A.M. we left for the airport. We left Durban on Air Rhodesia—a Friendship propjet where the wings are above the windows. The flight took 65 minutes to Lourenco Marques, Mozanbique. We checked into the Polana Hotel where we had lunch. Afternoon was at leisure. I went down to the hotel pool, but it was a little too cold for swimming. Dinner was at the hotel. Then Tony, Charles, Jane, and I went to town and got a beer.

July 17. After breakfast we had a free morning so I did try out the hotel pool. At 3:00 P.M. we began a city sightseeing tour where we drove along the Polana Beach to the Vasco de Gama Botanical Gardens. Then we visited the city hall, the cathedral, the Alvaro de Castro Museum with animals, the Yacht Club, and the modern St. Anthony's Church. As usual dinner was at the hotel.

July 18. After breakfast we had a leisurely drive in cars. We entered South Africa and Kruger National Park, destined for the Skukuza or Lower Sabie Rest Camps. We lunched at Lower Sabie; then we returned to Kruger National Park for the first of our game runs. Kruger is a world famous sanctuary where the wild animals live as they did before the arrival of man. We saw waterbuck, Cape buffalo, wart hogs, impalas, giraffes, elephants, baboons, kudus, vervet monkeys, zebras and steenbok. After our first game run we returned to Skukuza Park for lodging and dinner. The park gates are closed from 5:30 P.M. to 6:30 A.M. A fine is charged for late arrivals. Here is life in reverse. The animals are free, and the tourists are locked up.

July 19. Breakfast was at the Lodge, the Lower Sabie Rest Camp. We then left right away for our next game run, where we saw hyenas and lions eating a buffalo kill. This was not a very successful game run. We then returned to Skukuza Park for lunch. At 2:00 P.M. we drove to the park exit where we saw a zebra kill. A leopard had killed a baby zebra and had dragged it high in the tree. We also saw a sable antelope. We drove to Bushman Rock Hotel where we had access to a room for cleaning up before dinner. Dinner was at the hotel; then we left the hotel at 8:30 P.M. and drove to Nelspruit to board our train for Pretoria. We had tickets for train 8389, compartment A. Our berths were not made up, and we had to wait for mattresses. Our entire night was spent on the train.

July 20. Our train arrived in Pretoria at 7:30 A.M. We then drove in taxis to the Union Hotel where we had breakfast. Our individual rooms were not yet ready so the hotel supplied us with a suite for our temporary convenience. At 9:00 A.M. we left the hotel for our city sightseeing tour. We visited the Kruger House and saw the Voortrekker Museum. We returned to the hotel for lunch. At 2:00 P.M. we left the hotel again for the N'Debele Village to see the Mapoch Tribe. There was no dancing, but we did get to see their wares.

Afterwards we returned to the hotel for dinner. Later I wrote lots of postcards and sent lots of aerograms.

July 21. After breakfast we left at 7:30 for the airport. We flew Air Rhodesia, leaving at 9:30 A.M. and arriving at 11:30 A.M. at Bulawayo-Livingstone. Then we drove immediately to the Victoria Hotel where we had a box lunch, which we took with us to Matopos Park. We hiked to the top of the hill to see Cecil Rhodes' grave. It was terribly windy on top. Then we went to see the 2000-year-old paintings and prehistoric drawings at the Nswatugi Cave. A Matabele tribesman was the caretaker. We viewed the animal and human figures depicted in the bushman rock paintings. We then returned to the hotel for dinner. Charles and I went to the theatre to see "Funeral In Berlin".

July 22. After breakfast I went shopping with Charles. I got several local souvenirs. Also I was looking for Robert Ruark's book, *Something of Value*, but I couldn't find it. After lunch back at the hotel, our group left the hotel at 12:30 P.M. to go to the airport. Our flight on Air Rhodesia left at 1:40 P.M. and lasted one hour. We landed in Rhodesia where we were booked into the Victoria Falls Hotel, which is located right next to the falls. (Photo #35)

Photo #35

At the hotel a local family awaited us. The husband was the American councilman from Salisbury. He and his wife invited our group to their home for dinner. For dinner we had wine, prawns, and crepes Suzette. Afterwards we went to the casino. The entry fee was $3.00, and there was a $3.00 minimum of chips.

July 23. After breakfast we left the hotel at 10:00 A.M. for the African Craft Village and the Curio Shop. Then we toured the falls and got wet. Lunch was at the hotel. At 2:30 we left the hotel for the Zambesi River Cruise to Kandahar Island. The river has it source in Zambia, and it is the longest river that flows into the Indian Ocean. The most beautiful part of the river is Victoria Falls. On the island we got off to have tea and cookies. The island was checked first for elephants since they were seen there the preceding day. Returning to the hotel, we did see three elephants on George VI Island. Dinner as usual was at the hotel.

July 24. At 9:50 A.M. after breakfast we left the hotel for a charter flight over the beautiful Victoria Falls. The cost was an additional $4.28 and took 30 minutes. Lunch was at the hotel. Afterwards we left for the airport. This time it was an Air Rhodesia flight to Wankie. The flight took 30 minutes and landed right in the Wankie Reserve at the main camp. The giraffes were just off the landing field. The flight was very bumpy, and the aisle of the plane was the narrowest yet. We checked into Lodge C2. There was no electricity, but there was a Coleman lantern and 2 oil lamps. It had yellow bath fixtures and a completely new thatched roof. There was a refrigerator and stove. In the afternoon we went on another game run. Our dinner was at the Lodge. Afterwards they showed three movies on Rhodesia. We were in the open air surrounded by fires.

July 25. Breakfast was at the lodge. At 8:00 A.M. we left for a 4-hour game run. We returned to the main camp for lunch. In the afternoon our plane, Air Rhodesia, landed for us. We had a 1 hour, 15 minute ride to Kariba. We had a small plane, and I got permission to enter the cockpit and take pictures of Kariba Dam. Then we flew 1 hour 10 minutes more to Salisbury. We checked in to the Meikle's Hotel. Our dinner was in the Fontaine Room at the hotel.

July 26. Breakfast was at the hotel. We left for the city sightseeing tour of Salisbury. We visited the Queen Victoria Museum, then the Archives, then through the University of Salisbury. We also had a drive up the Koppie (a small hill) for the beautiful view of the city. Lunch was at the hotel in the main dining room. At 2:30 P.M. we left for a visit of the Emerald Factory featuring the Sandawana Emeralds. They are considered one of the best in the world and rivals of the Columbian emeralds. The mine was discovered in 1956. Afterwards, we got to shop. Dinner that evening was with Bill and Judy Clair, the American consul in Rhodesia. Their house was in the Highlands. She served Chinese food. Mel Brooks and his wife were there from Nairobi.

July 27. I skipped breakfast today and went to the post office to mail my numerous tour pamphlets home. I then bought 4 souvenir ashtrays and had them also shipped home along with my Ashanti fertility dolls. My purchase in Ghana of the fertility dolls was considered a waste of my money by my tour companions, but as the tour progressed, they became an object of desire. On several occasions tour members asked me if I would sell them one of my dolls, and I always refused.

Lunch was at La Fontaine. Since Salisbury has a great program set up to greet the tourists, groups of us were assigned to local members of the community. At 3:00 P.M. Frank Henderson, a local businessman, met my roommate Jane and me in the lobby, and we drove to Urinenri about 20 miles away. Then we stopped at his home in the Highlands for a Sundowner. He invited Jane, our guide Tony, and me to dinner at the Salisbury Club, a members only club. We had mushroom soup, chicken and peas, white wine, coffee, and Grand Marnier.

July 28. Our breakfast this morning was served in our room because we had to leave early. We left the hotel at 7:30 A.M. Our Air Rhodesia flight left at 8:15 A.M. and lasted

1 hour 30 minutes. Our destination was Blantyre, Malawi. At Blantyre we had city sightseeing and 100 miles of country sightseeing. Then our flight to Dar Es Salaam took another 1 hour 30 minutes. We had lunch at the Malawi airport. We checked into the Kilimanjaro Hotel, a lovely hotel. Dinner was at the Summit Room at the hotel.

July 29. After breakfast as usual we left for the city sightseeing. We stopped at the local market, but this was not a good experience since there were so many bad smells there. Then we drove through the university, the beach, and finally the museum where we saw the Zinjanthropus skull, a million+ year old skull discovered by Mary and Louis Leakey in the '50's. We returned to the hotel for lunch. Our afternoon was at leisure so I chose to go shopping with Charles. Dinner was at the hotel roof garden with music. Later I had a Kilimanjaro Beer.

July 30. We had another early breakfast at the hotel since we were scheduled for an early flight. We caught the 7:30 A.M. flight to the island of Zanzibar. The flight lasted only 15 minutes. We had a second breakfast at the Zanzibar Hotel. Then we toured the island—the Arab Fort, the Sultans' Palace, and the Anglican Church which was built on the site of the old slave market. We returned to the hotel for lunch and then left for the airport. The plane left at 2:40 P.M. and arrived at Mombasa, Kenya, at 4:00 P.M. We checked in at the Oceanic Hotel. The hotel was modern but the noisiest ever. The afternoon was free, but we were far from the city proper. Dinner was at the hotel with music.

July 31. After breakfast the city sightseeing tour included the Wailing Mosque, the old harbor, a museum, and Fort

Jesus. We spent one hour shopping before returning to the hotel for lunch. At 2:00 P.M. we left for a native village, then Oceanic's Private Beach. At the native market, I bought a hand-carved wart hog and rhino plus 2 more statues, all four of which I sent home. We returned to the hotel by taxi for dinner.

Photo #36

August 1. After breakfast we left the hotel at 8:30 A.M. for a 10:00 flight to Moshi via Eastern African Airlines. The flight lasted 45 minutes. After landing, we drove 50 miles to Arusha. Lunch was at the new Arusha Hotel. We left the hotel at 2:00 P.M. and drove 75 miles to Lake Manyara National Park. En route we passed several Masai Warriors. (Photo #36) We checked in at the Lake Manyara Hotel and had dinner at the hotel. Lake Manyara is located at the foot of the Great Rift Wall. The National Park located here is famous for its lions in the trees. Dinner was at the hotel.

August 2. After breakfast we left for a morning game run in the Lake Manyara National Park. I got a wonderful picture of a leopard and a lion in the tree. We returned to the hotel for lunch. Afterwards we drove 48 miles to the Ngorongoro Crater, the most spectacular crater in the world. We checked into the Ngorongoro Crater Lodge which sits on the rim of the crater. Dinner at the lodge was wildebeest steak, which was delicious.

Photo #37

August 3. We left the Lodge at 7:30 A.M. after breakfast for an all-day game run. Within 30 minutes we had descended to the floor of the crater. Land Rovers are used for the game runs. (Photo #37) There is a lot of dust on the crater floor and practically no road. We saw lions, lionesses, black rhinos, Thompson and Grant Gazelles, zebras, wildebeest, crested cranes, and secretary birds. At the Crater

Lake there were flocks of flamingos. At lunchtime we had a picnic in the Garden of Eden with box lunches packed by the Lodge. The Lodge is 6,000 feet above the crater, and it took more than one hour to reach the crater floor. We returned to the Lodge at 3:30 P.M. after viewing several hippos, 2 rhinos and 1 lion. We arrived at the Lodge exhausted. Dinner at the Lodge was roast leg of wildebeest, which was not nearly as good as the wildebeest steak that I had before.

August 4. After breakfast we were divided into two groups, and each group chartered a Travcoa bus and drove to Oldevai Gorge, which was 40 minutes away. Olduvai Gorge is a steep-sided ravine in the Great Rift Valley that stretches through eastern Africa. It is in the eastern Serengeti Plains in northern Tanzania. The purpose of this trip was to see Dr. Leakey's excavations of the Zinjanthropus Man. Zinjanthropus Man is Arabic for East African Man. Olduvai is Masai for the Sisal Plant growing everywhere. After visiting the 2 sites, we returned to the Ngorongoro Crater at 12:00 noon for lunch. At 1:30 P.M., we left the Lodge for a long 3-hour drive to Arusha, Tanganyika. We stopped at the outskirts of the city to visit a Masai Market. Then we checked in to the New Arusha Hotel. Dinner as usual was at the hotel.

August 5. At 8:00 A.M. after breakfast we left the hotel for Amboseli, Kenya, where we stayed in lodges. The lodges are new and rent for $35.00 a night. For lunch we had a cold buffet before leaving for another game run. This time we saw a lioness and 2 rhinos in the thicket. We had cocktails before dinner in the colonel's room just next door to our room. Just before sunset we got a spectacular view of Mt. Kilimanjaro.

After dinner we had coffee outside the lodges before an open fire.

August 6. After breakfast at the Lodge, we had a morning game run, and then we left on a 92-mile ride to Nairobi. Half of the distance was over very rough roads. We arrived at the New Stanley Hotel just before lunch. In the afternoon we went to the post office to mail pamphlets home, then finished the afternoon with shopping. Dinner was at the hotel in celebration of H. Adams birthday, one of our participants.

August 7. After breakfast we left the hotel for the animal orphanage where we saw several cheetahs and a leopard. It's just like one big zoo. Then we drove thru the Nairobi National Park, 44 square miles just outside Nairobi. I photographed the hartebeest and a pride of lions on the way back to the hotel. We stopped at the Wild Life Office at Wilson Airport where I ordered 35 Christmas cards plus two calendars. I also bought 20 Christmas cards. The cards were 14 cents each and the calendars were $2.00 each. After lunch at the hotel, I went to the post office to mail my cards home. Then we shopped all afternoon. I also stopped at the TWA office and confirmed my flight home from New York to Cincinnati on the 25th at 4:15 P.M. Dinner at the hotel was in the bar. I had to completely organize my suitcases in order to take only one suitcase to Tree Tops. I left the other 2 at the hotel. Then when I returned, I would pick up one more for Uganda and leave the small one at the hotel.

A really funny story developed from this day until the next morning. Charles decided that he no longer needed one of his heavy jackets. Since one of the porters at the hotel had been extremely nice and friendly to him, Charles decided to leave him a gift of his jacket. The porter had shined his shoes and had been very attentive so the next morning prior to leaving, Charles gave his jacket to the porter. It didn't take long before chaos broke out. It seems that there was a hierarchy among the hotel staff. The porter at the top of the ladder found out that one of the porters beneath him had received a gift. According to local tradition the porter at the top of the ladder must receive the gift. It did not matter that he had done nothing for you. He was the most important one so he claimed the jacket for himself. After a long discussion and to make everyone happy, Charles had to buy his jacket back from the receiver so that he could give it to the person at the top of the chain. Thereby everyone was happy. Our porter had a gift of money, and the top ranking porter had a jacket. All of this had to be settled before we left the hotel. One never really knows the local customs.

August 8. After breakfast and the difficulty with the jacket, we left the hotel at 9:30 A.M. for a 92-mile ride to Treetops. Then we drove to the Outspan Hotel in Nyeri where all the tours to Treetops originate. We had a cold buffet lunch on the porch at the hotel. Then we had to wait until 3:00 P.M. for our Treetops Tour. There was a nice gift shop in the Ourspan Hotel so we spent our extra time shopping. At the exact time we drove to Treetops, about 10 miles away, in land rovers over a dirt road. Treetops Hotel is very interesting. Upon arrival you must exit the land rover, then under the watch of an armed guide, the last 100 yards must be walked in the company of this armed guard. He carried a 470 rifle, which is powerful enough to kill anything.

Treetops Hotel is fantastic. There were exactly 23 rooms built high up in a tree in Aberdare National Park in Kenya. Today it has been expanded again to more than 45 rooms. It is in sight of Mount Kenya. The rooms for our stay rented for about $35.00 each. We had Room #23 which was one of the best. It overlooked the waterhole which is the reason that we were at this hotel—to see the animals at night drinking at the waterhole. One of the interesting facts about the hotel is that Princess Elizabeth was staying there when her father George VI died. So she went up the tree as a princess and came down the tree as Queen of England. Treetops has a nice platform to watch the animals and most of the watch was done at night when the animals went to the water hole to drink. (Photo #38)

Photo #38

All the food at Treetops had to be driven in and hoisted up to us. At 4:30 we had afternoon tea, scones, and cake. Dinner at 8:00 P.M. was asparagus, cream of chicken soup, marrow, roast beef, fruit salad, cheese, and coffee. Afterwards we saw 54 elephants, 42 buffalo, 4 rhino, 3 white-tailed mongeese, and 2 waterbuck. Everyone at Treetops kept an exact count of the animals viewed. We could see all the activity at the waterhole from our observation porch. (Photo #39)

Photo #39

August 9. We got up at 6:45 A.M. Tea was served in the Treetops Bar. At 7:30 A.M. we left Treetops in the care of the hunter and walked through lots of mud to get to the land rover. Then we drove 10 miles to the Outspan Hotel in Nyeri. We first cleaned our shoes and legs, and then we had breakfast at the hotel. At 9:00 A.M. we left the hotel for a 92-mile trip back to Nairobi. A smorgasbord lunch was at the New Stanley Hotel. They served us the most delicious pastries. We had time for shopping in the afternoon before we left at 5:00 P.M. for the airport. We had dinner at the airport. Our plane was to have been a Friendship EAA Fokker, leaving at 7:00 P.M., landing at 8:30 P.M. Instead we got an EAA Comet Jet that made the trip in one hour. On the flight I bought a bourbon and coke for $.70. We landed in Entebbe, Uganda and drove 25 miles to the Apollo Hotel in Kampala, capital of Uganda.

August 10. We left the Apollo after breakfast at 9:30 A.M. for a 260-mile drive to Queen Elizabeth Park, Uganda. En route we stopped for lunch at the Tropic Inn in Masaka, 81 miles away. Afterwards we had a 180-mile ride over many dirt roads to reach our quarters at Mweya Safari Lodge, Queen Elizabeth Park. The lodge is on the Mweya Peninsula that has a great view high on a bluff overlooking the Kazinga Channel. Dinner was at 7:30. Afterwards I found ants in our hotel room so I had to fumigate for them.

August 11. After breakfast we left the hotel at 8:45 for our morning launch trip. Our motor launch left at 9:00 for a trip up the Kazinga Channel linking Lake Edward and Lake George. It's famous for its bird life and scenery. We did see lots of birds plus hundreds of hippos, also 4 hyenas, some elephants and buffalo. We returned to the pier at noon. At 3:30 we left for an afternoon game run, where we saw 20 lions and a lot more hippos in the mud, also waterbuck and warthogs. Dinner at the Mweya Lodge was terrible.

August 12. The morning's trip was a 70-mile trek past the Mountains of the Moon to Fort Portal where we checked into the Mountains of the Moon Hotel. We were scheduled to visit the primitive village of the Bambouti Pygmies with permission to photograph. The Bambouti Pygmies are located on the edge of the famed Ituri Forest. En route, we passed a sign that cautioned the tourists that this was a dangerous area. However our guide assured us that there was no problem with the pygmies. (Photo #40)

Photo #40

En route we ate our box lunches that the hotel had prepared for us. The mountains are called Ruwenzori known by the ancients as the Mountains of the Moon. The trip to the village was 45 miles

When we arrived at the village, we were met by the local pygmies. But the reception was not a friendly one. They threatened to stone us if we didn't pay a ransom to photograph them whether we wanted to take pictures or not.

Carole J. Kuhn, Ph. D.

Therefore we had to pass a hat around to ransom ourselves. On the first pass of the hat, the pygmies decided that there was not enough money so we had to pass the hat around again. The driver collected the money and gave it to the pygmies so that we could take photographs. This was certainly a scary situation. We were only 12 among a group of really smelly natives so we had no bargaining rights. The ransom amounted to a little more than $30.00, but that was a lot of money at that time for the local pygmies. The pygmies really smelled bad, and we kept the windows closed most of the time in spite of the terrible heat. Many of them were smoking marijuana and drinking concoctions made of the narcotic. They asked for many things in addition to the ransom money—pens, books, maps of Uganda, and lipstick. (Photo #41)

Photo #41

Needless to say we did not spend much time in the Mountains of the Moon. After this experience we drove back to the Mountains of the Moon Hotel for dinner and rest after a very taxing day.

August 13. Our morning visit was to a tea plantation, then a return to the hotel for lunch. We left the hotel at 1:15 P.M. after a group picture. Our afternoon was a 160-mile drive to Masindi where we checked into the Masindi Hotel for dinner and an overnight stay. Masindi is on the road to Murchison Falls which was our next destination. Dinner was mediocre.

August 14. At 9:00 A.M. we left the hotel and drove 70 miles to Chobe Falls located in Murchison Falls National Park. En route we stopped at Karuma Bridge to view the White Nile which starts in Lake Victoria. Karuma Bridge is considered the gateway to northern Uganda. Our hotel was the Chobe Safari Lodge which is on the banks of the Nile. At 3:00 P.M. we left for an afternoon game run. We saw a few elephants, many giraffes, lots of warthogs, a bushbuck, and a sausage tree. Our game run lasted 3 hours. When we returned to the Lodge, several tour members gave me an advanced Birthday Party at dinner.

August 15. We left the hotel at 9:00 A.M. and drove 70 miles to the Paraa Safari Lodge, located just inside Murchison Falls National Park. En route we saw several wildlife animals. At 2:00 P.M. we boarded a launch for a cruise on the White Nile all the way to Murchison Falls. We passed lots of crocodiles and hippos. We also saw many elephants, buffalo, hartebeest, waterbuck, and Colobus Monkeys which resemble skunks because they are black and white. We returned to the lodge for dinner, which featured Nile Perch. The Lodge had two local elephants which frequented the area. I fed candy to one of them.

August 16. After breakfast we left the lodge for a 200-mile drive. Our first stop was Murchison Falls where we took a ferry across the Nile. We climbed to the top of the hill overlooking the falls. Then we drove to Masindi where we had lunch at the Masindi Hotel. The hotel has two Colobus monkeys. After lunch we drove thru Kampala to Entebbe and the Lake Victoria Hotel. The airport was our next destination. We flew East Africa Airways back to Nairobi in just one hour and checked in at the New Stanley Hotel.

August 17. Early coffee was sent to the room, and we left at 7:00 A.M. for the airport. Our flight left at 8:45. At 9:05 we flew over the Equator on Ethiopian Airlines. The flight lasted 1 hour 30 minutes. We checked in at the Ghion Hotel in Addis Ababa, Ethiopia. Part of the hotel was new and part was old. Since the Nigerian-Biafra Meetings were being held in Addis Ababa, the important participants were housed in the new part, and our group was put in the old part. The old part was terrible. After lunch we left on a city sightseeing tour. We viewed the old market, then the new market, then to the palace to see Haile Selasie's pet cheetahs, then to the city lion cages, where they have about 10 lions, then to the museum, then to Mt. Entot, the highest panoramic view overlooking the city of Addis Ababa. Dinner later was at the hotel.

August 18. This day was totally at leisure. I had breakfast with Charles, and then we skipped lunch and walked downtown to see a movie. We saw Charles Boyer and Lilie Palmer in *Love and Kisses* with Rickie and Christine Nelson. Dinner later was at the hotel.

August 19. At 9:30 A.M. we left the hotel to catch our Ethiopian Jet 720 to Asmara, a 55-minute flight. Our flight took us over the mountains, and there was a lot of turbulence on the flight. I had never bounced around so much on a huge jet. When we landed we drove to the Asmara Imperial Hotel for lunch. A friend of mine had a sister who lived in Asmara so after lunch I made plans to visit her and her family the following day after the Red Sea visit. We left the hotel at 2:30 and drove almost 3 hours thru the rain and the mountains to the Red Sea—a descent of 8,000 feet. The temperature at the Red Sea was 120 degrees. We checked into the Red Sea Hotel where we relaxed and had dinner.

August 20. At 9:00 we left the hotel for morning sightseeing. Then we drove 7 kilometers to the beach, and then returned to the hotel for lunch. At 2:00 P.M. we left in our bus for the return visit to Asmara. About 10 miles from the city our bus broke down. My friends in Asmara were waiting my arrival for a delayed birthday party. Since we would only be in Asmara two nights, I felt obligated to do something. So I asked Jean and Helen, two participants on our trip, if they would get off the bus and hitchhike with me back to Asmara. They didn't want me to go alone, so they decided to accompany me. The first passing car stopped to pick us up. Inside were two Ethiopian navy military personnel. They were extremely friendly and were intent on practicing their English.

We got back to the city before the 6:00 gates closed. Our bus that had broken down arrived two hours later. I immediately called my hosts, and they picked me up at the hotel. I spent the evening with them for drinks and dinner, and I stayed at their home for the night. When I got back home, my friends thought I was crazy to hitchhike in Ethiopia because Americans were thought to be very rich, and we were traveling though a poor country. We could have been robbed or killed, but the world was a different place at that time. In today's world, I would never do that again.

August 21. After breakfast and lunch, we left the hotel in a land rover for sightseeing. This was a day at leisure for us so I didn't miss anything while visiting with my friends. The husband was stationed at the nearby base so we called our guide Tony, and invited him to join us for dinner at the NCO Club on base. Afterwards we visited three different houses for drinks. I spent the second night with my friends.

August 22. I spent the morning with my friends, and they took me to the airport at 2:00 P.M. for a 2:30 flight to Kasala. We had to pass customs in Kasala, and in order to pass customs, everything was pulled off the plane by the custom officials. This proved to be much ado about nothing. Then we all reboarded the plane for another hour and a half flight to Khartoum, Sudan. Although we had already passed customs, we still had a one-hour delay for our luggage. We checked in at the Grand Hotel in Khartoum. In the evening Tony, our guide, had a party in his room. This was Charles' last night so he was busy packing. Tony and I took a long walk along the Nile.

August 23. We left the hotel after breakfast for sightseeing, but told Charles good-bye before leaving. We saw where the two Niles come together, then the old market, the animal market, and a museum with General Gordon's personal things. We also saw the old Dervish Forts in the distance. I skipped lunch because the food was terrible. At 9:00 P.M. we left for the airport. There was a delay at the airport since this was the end of our trip, and we could not check in as a group. Everyone weighed in separately, and almost everyone sent his luggage on to N.Y. The plane left at 11:00 P.M. for a 2 hour 15 minute flight to Cairo. The plane was Misrair-United Arab Airlines. We arrived at Cairo at 4:00 A.M. There was a one-hour time change. Immediately we checked into the Nile Hilton Hotel.

August 24. I got to sleep three hours, and then had breakfast at the hotel. Our guide, Tony, did not come to the airport with us. I got an Air France flight #125 to Athens (1 hour 20 minutes), then a 3 hour 15 minute flight to Paris. I had a four-hour layover at Orly. Then I was booked on Air France flight 017 to New York. The flight was only 1/5 full, about 40 passengers. As usual my friend picked me up at the greater Cincinnati airport when I arrived home.

Chapter Eight

1969 Travel-a-Go-go Tour

The following year in 1969 I found a local travel group called Travel-a-Go-go. This local group had chartered a plane for this experience. It was located on Reading Road in Cincinnati, and it offered a spring tour that coincided with my spring break. It was April 3 through April 7 and promised a long weekend in Guatemala. A tourist card was needed for the Guatemalan visit. The total flight cost was only $128.00 on Flight #112. We were to spend the Easter weekend in Guatemala. The Ground Package at the Hotel "El Camino Real" was $52.00 if we shared a room and $75.00 if we wanted a single.

This plane included a lot of local people who had previously traveled with this group so many of them were familiar with one another. I felt very much an outsider since I knew no one in the group. We were to leave on Thursday late afternoon from the Greater Cincinnati Airport, and when we were on board and ready to leave, an announcement was made that we were waiting for one passenger who had not yet arrived. This was a long time before cell phones so it was difficult to contact him from the plane. The missing member was a local dentist who lived in Hamilton, Ohio, and who usually traveled with the group. We waited, and we waited. Finally after many attempts to reach him, we left the airport without him, and flew to Guatemala City. Our meal on the plane included complimentary champagne and dinner. We arrived in Guatemala City at 8:15 P.M. and set our watches back one hour. Our hotel in Guatemala City was the Hotel Camino Real.

April 4. Today was Holy Friday, and we had an all-day tour to Antigua where we saw the ruins of the Capuchinas Monastery and the Good Friday procession throughout the city. We had lunch at the Hotel Antigua.

April 5. We arranged a 60-minute flight to Tikal, the capital city of the Mayan empire where we saw the famous temple pyramids rising out of the dense Peten jungle. Especially important was the Giant Jaguar Pyramid. We also got to visit the Palace of the Nobles. It is still a mystery today why this capital city of the Mayan empire sank into oblivion, but it still remains a fascinating archaeological site.

April 6. We drove to Chichicastenango and the magnificent Lake Atitlan, advertised as the "world's most beautiful lake". The twelve villages around the mile-high lake are named for the twelve Apostles. We got to shop in the large open-air Indian market and watch the religious ceremonies at the church of Santo Tomas. We visited the home of the Indian mask makers and walked up the mountain trails. Lunch was at the Hotel Casa Contenta.

April 7. We departed from Guatemala City at 3:00 P.M. and arrived in Cincinnati at 10:15 P.M. During the entire trip everyone wondered what had happened to the local dentist who was supposed to be on the trip with us. Only when we returned did we learn that the local Hamilton dentist had been murdered the night before our trip, and that explained why he hadn't made the trip with us. I did not know the dentist, but everyone on the trip seemed to know him. In retrospect, that was so unusual—sitting on a plane waiting for someone who had been murdered.

Chapter Nine

1969-70 Compass Christmas Tour To the Soviet Union and Czechoslovakia

The dead of winter was a special time to visit the U.S.S.R. and Czechoslovakia. The trip was promoted as a medical and educational tour, and it coincided with the Moscow Winter Theatrical Festival. On Friday, December 19, 1969, I boarded a TWA flight #152 from Dayton, Ohio, to Kennedy Airport where the Compass Group assembled prior to our flight. Then we boarded Pan American flight #44 which departed at 7:45 P.M.

December 20. We arrived in Copenhagen and then changed planes leaving on Aeroflot Flight #1145 to Leningrad. We arrived in Leningrad at 7:30 P.M.

December 21. Our sightseeing of Leningrad included Nevsky Prospect, the Admiralty Building, the Pushkin Theatre, Peter and Paul Fortress, and St. Isaacs's Cathedral. Also we visited the Winter Palace, and the Hermitage Museum, famous for its paintings collected by Catherine the Great. In the evening we saw *The Blue Danube* Ballet by Johann Strauss.

December 22. After breakfast we left for a school visitation—grades 1-10, School #169 specializing in English. The various grades entertained us with folk dancing and

American and Russian songs. They presented each one of us with a wooden doll and a postcard. After lunch we took a tour of Peter and Paul Fortress and Cathedral to see where all the tsars are buried. After dinner we went to the Circus.

Photo #42

December 23. We had a half-day educational program in Leningrad about its history and its problems in the wars. In the afternoon we had time to visit the stores on Nevsky Prospect. Since this was the Christmas season there was evidence of this all around the country. The Russian Communist Party did not believe in Christianity, but they did accept a figure called Ded Moroz (Дед Мороз) or Father Frost. He usually would arrive in the company of the Snow Maiden, and the two of them would distribute gifts to the children. They usually made their visits during the New Year's celebrations. I must admit Father Frost looked a lot like Santa Claus. (Photo #42) We ended up at the Anti-religious Exhibit at the Museum of the History of Religion at Kazan Cathedral. They capitalized on the Inquisition and tortures plus the difference between the starving masses and the elite clergy.

December 24. This morning we traveled to Pushkin, formerly Tsarskoe Selo, the site of Catherine the Great's beautiful palace. Of special notice were large black and white photos of the palace in ruins as the Nazis left it during the war. The photos emphasized all of the work that the Russians had to do to make the palace beautiful again. Also nearby we visited Pavlovsk, the youngest of the grand imperial estates around St. Petersburg. This neo-classical palace and its extensive landscaped gardens were built in honor of Tsar Pavel (Paul). Pushkin was much more impressive. We boarded Aeroflot Flight #3843 at 6:05 P.M. for our flight to Kiev, where we landed at 7:55 P.M. Kiev is much colder than Leningrad. Due to delays we didn't get to our hotel until midnight. My suitcase arrived with a large tear in it.

December 25. Christmas Day. We had lots of city sightseeing including the Golden Gates of the 11th century fortress. It was so cold that the bus windows were frosted up, and it was difficult to see out. We also visited the tomb of Yaroslav the Wise, St. Sophia, and The Kievo-Pechersk Monastery-The Lavra, known as the Monastery of the Caves. Yaroslav the Wise, was an 11th century ruler of Kiev. St. Sophia was a second century saint important in the Eastern Orthodox Church. At 5:15 P.M. we left the hotel to go to St. Vladimir's Church for a Russian Orthodox Mass.

December 26. In the morning we had a class on the history of Kiev. In the afternoon we visited a Young pioneer Palace.

December 27. After breakfast we went to visit Babi Yar, a ravine where the Nazis massacred the townspeople of Kiev during World War II. It holds a special place in the hearts of the people of Kiev. The ravine was filled in, but it contains the bodies of tens of thousands of Jews and townspeople of Kiev. We left Kiev on Aeroflot Flight #870 at 11:53 A.M. for a flight to Moscow, arriving at 1:38 P.M. We checked in at the Rossia Hotel. After dinner we walked around Red Square and watched the changing of the guard at Lenin's tomb. At the Service Bureau we got tickets to the *Nutcracker Suite* at the Bolshoi Theatre for the 28th.

December 28. Our Moscow sightseeing included places of historical interest, architectural monuments, new buildings, and projects under construction. We did visit the U.S.S.R. Exhibition of Economic Achievements. The highlight of our sightseeing was a visit to the famous Tretyakov Art Gallery. This gallery differs from the Hermitage in that it features Russian artists, not the famous French or Italian ones. At the Tretyakov one finds a beautiful icon collection. I especially liked Andrei Rublev's icon of *The Trinity*. Then there was *The Virgin of Vladimir*, a 12th century icon. The Tretyakov also featured many Russian 19th century painters such as I.E. Repin, A.K. Savrasov, V.G. Perov, A.A. Ivanov, V.A. Serov, and O.A. Kiprensky. The evening was spent at the Bolshoi Theatre.

December 29. Today was an all-day visit to the Kremlin to view the historical and architectural monuments: the ancient cathedrals of the Assumption, the Church of Coronations and Marriages, Michel, the Archangel—where the tsars are buried—and the Deposition of the Robe, in addition to the Ivan the Great Bell Tower and the Annunciation Cathedral. (Photo #43)

Photo #43

In addition, no visit to the Kremlin would be complete without a visit to the Kremlin Armory to see the Russian Imperial Jewels and a display of ten of the Imperial Easter Eggs designed by Fabergé. There was also a visit to Vladimir Lenin's Tomb. The tomb was guarded by two Soviet soldiers, and there was a strict observance of silence when entering. No talking whatsoever was allowed. Also no photos were ever allowed of the soviet leader. His embalmed body has been on public display there since his death in 1924. In the evening we went to the Bolshoi Theatre for a performance of *Giselle*, a ballet by A. Adan.

December 30. Today was an educational study program concerning the history of Moscow. Later in the day we visited Sokolniki Park. Peter the Great named it after his love of falcons. While there we were treated to Troika rides through the park. (Photo #44) In the evening we went to the Tchaikovsky Theatre to see the Moiseyev Dancers—considered the best folk dancing anywhere. It was directed by Igor Moiseyev, himself.

Photo #44

December 31. We left for a day trip from Moscow to Zagorsk, the spiritual center of the Greek Orthodox Church, about 60 miles from Moscow. We visited the Monastery, featuring the Cathedral of the Assumption. The cathedral is within the walls of the Trinity-Sergius Monastery and was founded in 1345 by St. Sergius of Radonezh and contains his relics. We returned to Moscow for a fantastic New Year's Eve Party which was a 6-hour feast. It began at 11:00 P.M. and had six separate courses all served with various wines. It continued until 5:00 A.M., but I left at 2:00 A.M. after many rounds of Russian singing. I knew many of the songs so I could join right in. You become instantaneous friends if you can sing their songs.

January 1. We left Moscow on Aeroflot Flight #085 at 8:20 A.M. for a flight to Prague. We arrived there at 9:10 A.M., checked into the International Hotel, and then had a study program on what to expect in Prague.

January 2. Today included lots of sightseeing beginning with the Old Town, followed by the Charles Bridge, St. Nicholas Church, and St. Vitas Cathedral, where Prince Wenceslas is buried. Later we visited Strahov Stadium, the Wallenstein Garden, and the old Jewish Synagogue and Cemetery. The architecture of Prague is mostly Rococo and Baroque.

January 3. We left Prague for a flight to Frankfurt. Then we took Pan American Flight #77 at 3:00 P.M. direct to New York, arriving at Kennedy Airport at 7:30 P.M. Then I connected to TWA Flight #3, leaving Kennedy at 11:15 P.M. arriving Cincinnati 1:05 A. M.

Chapter Ten

1971 Russian Language Study Tour

This 1971 summer tour was in conjunction with Southern Illinois University at Carbondale.

June 21. I left Cincinnati on a flight to St. Louis, and then transferred to a chartered jet to London Heathrow with a stopover in New York.

June 22-July 2. We checked in to the Queen's Garden Hotel in London, and for the next 2 weeks we would be studying Russian history while enjoying sightseeing in London and waiting for our ship to arrive. I had a roommate, Chris, who shared a double room with me; however our hotel was a real "dive". We had no toilet and no shower in our room.

While in London we saw all the standard tourist spots—the British Museum, the Tower of London, Westminster Abbey, Hampton Court Palace, Windsor, the Tate Gallery, St. Paul's Cathedral and Buckingham Palace. We also visited many sites outside London, Winchester Cathedral, Salisbury Cathedral, Stonehenge, Canterbury Cathedral, Stratford-on-Avon with Shakespeare's home, and nearby Anne Hatheway's cottage, plus Warwick Castle. One day I caught a boat to Kew Gardens.

July 2. At 10:00 we boarded a bus and left for Tillbury where we boarded the Russian steamer *Alexander Pushkin* for a five-day cruise of the North and Baltic Seas on our way to Leningrad. On board we had Russian lessons every day. En route we docked in Bremerhaven, Germany, where we had a walking tour of the city.

July 6. We docked in Helsinki, Finland. In Helsinki we had a three-hour mini tour of the city and environs. We had culture classes on board the *Pushkin* while waiting for our arrival in Leningrad, and we also had lots of entertainment.

July 7-31. The Scheduled Intensive Language Program at the Poly-Technical Institute in Leningrad included 4-5 hours daily in class and six days a week of lectures and conferences. We landed at Leningrad, and the formalities took forever. I had three cameras, and they told me that three cameras were not allowed. So I had to give two of my cameras to my friends, just temporarily. Our housing was at the Leningrad Poly-Technical Institute, a branch of Leningrad State University.

We, as students, were in the hands of "Sputnik" Travel. As a regular tourist we would be in the hands of "Intourist" Travel, which is the highest level of Russian travel. "Sputnik" Travel left a lot to be desired. We did have separate rooms at the University, but the mattresses were paper thin and not too clean. My very first night on my mattress proved a disaster. The next morning when I got out of bed, my body was covered with red marks that I could not identify. When I checked around, I was told that they were bedbug bites from the insects inside my mattress. I immediately requested a change of mattresses. I think things like this happen because there are students from all over the world here in Leningrad studying, and there is no check on cleanliness.

A second item of concern was the quality of the food being served. The food with "Intourist" was top-notch. The food under the direction of "Sputnik" was marginal at best. At worst, it was inedible.

A third item of concern were the facilities. Our room was on the fourth floor, and the showers were in the basement. The toilets were at the other end of the building along with the washroom. However, I wanted to improve my Russian so I had to put up with these discomforts.

In addition to our classes, the days were loaded with seminars with academicians. After the classes we were treated to lots of tours of Leningrad and environs. During my study in Leningrad, I met another teacher named Natasha. She was a native of Leningrad, and she was teaching English. We developed a friendship since we could exchange ideas and methods of language learning. I will write more about Natasha later.

While in Leningrad we did visit Peterhof, Peter and Paul Fortress, and Piskarevsky Memorial Cemetery where about 500,000 people are buried. Most of the dead died of starvation during the 90-day Siege of Leningrad in World War II. The cemetery visit is made most impressive with the playing of Chopin's "Funeral March". Our next visit was to Kizhi and the beautiful Church of Transfiguration. Its architecture is unique, and the icon collection inside is magnificent. The visit to the Alexander Nevsky Monastery complex was especially interesting because it contained the Tikhvin Cemetery with the graves of many of the Russian masters: Dostoevsky, Mussorgsky Tchikovsky, Rubinstein, Glinka, and Rimsky-Korsakov.

Our group also had an opportunity to visit a camp of Young Pioneers near Leningrad. It was one of the many hundreds of summer camps in the U.S.S.R. We were also treated to a visit of Novgorod, a beautiful city of Russian domes, churches, and icons.

Later when I was teaching Russian, I would pick up on the idea of a Russian Camp like one of the many that I had visited in the U.S.S.R. Another high school Russian teacher, who taught nearby, and I would take our Russian students out on a weekend camping trip to a campground where we would attempt to imitate our own version of a Young Pioneer Camp. Our camp would be called Lager Druzhba, Friendship Camp. We would expose our students to Russian dancing, singing, and Russian themes. I would teach a class on Pysanky, the art of Ukrainian egg decoration. Also we would serve Russian food, and our students were encouraged to speak only Russian while at camp. Our Russian Camp, of course, was lacking in communist indoctrination.

Before we left the vicinity of Leningrad, we visited the royal village of Tsarskoye Selo which has now been renamed Pushkin to honor the Russian poet. It is located about 15 miles south of Leningrad and was the summer residence of the Russian tsars. The beautiful blue Catherine Palace is remarkable. At its entrance it also has the black and white photos showing the damage orchestrated by the Nazis during WW II.

August 1-5. We caught a train to Moscow, the capital of the Soviet Union. Here we had extensive sightseeing of the city as well as more seminars with more academicians. One special tourist visit was to the Rublev Monastery where there is a collection of his famous icons. A second special visit was to St. Basil's Church, usually just seen from a distance. One afternoon we visited the Tretyakov Gallery, the best place to view Russian art. We were still in the hands of "Sputnik", but our accommodations and food were better than before because we were traveling and not in the confines of the university.

August 6-9. We caught another train to Kiev, the capital of the Ukraine. As usual we had more lectures and lots of sightseeing in Kiev. The most famous place of interest in Kiev is St. Sophia's. While there, I took a two-hour river cruise on the Dnieper. Another afternoon we had a tour of the Shevchenko State Museum, Kiev's most famous poet.

August 9-13. This time our train took us to Yalta where we stayed with the Gurquf Youth Camp. These accommodations were still on par with "Sputnik", but this time we were in the South so in addition to sightseeing we had lots of time for sunbathing in the Black Sea.

August 13-15. Our group flew from Yalta to Odessa to board a Black Sea Cruise to Varna, Bulgaria. Varna is considered the sea capital of Bulgaria. In Varna we stayed overnight. Then we caught a flight back to Odessa. After some sightseeing and another boat trip, we ended up on the Potemkin Staircase. At one of the cafés nearby the waitress did not want to serve us. This was not the first time that a waitress reacted this way. It had happened also in Leningrad. Not serving the enemy was considered very patriotic by Big Brother during the Cold War. When that happens, you can move to another table or another restaurant. We got a boat back to Varna in preparation for the train to Belgrade.

August 16-21. We had some time in the morning for shopping, and I had purchased some crystal wine glasses to take home. We boarded the Orient Express at night for an overnight trip to Belgrade. We were put in a compartment for 6 people. About two hours into the trip, I needed something from my luggage which was stored in one of the upper racks, and John, one of the students in my compartment offered to help me. When he reached for the handle of my suitcase, he accidentally pulled the train's emergency cord. That made the train come to a full stop for inspection. This procedure delayed our trip by 30 minutes. That in and of itself was not too important at the time, but the ramifications of the delay would impact our trip.

Early the next morning before breakfast, as the train was speeding toward Belgrade, we felt a large jolt, and the train was derailed and came to a fast stop. It seems that we had hit something. The porters came thru the compartments and told everyone to pick up all our luggage and transport it to the next village which was about ¾ of a mile away. What we had hit was a very large bull. It seems that a farmer had let his bull out to pasture, a chore that he was used to doing every day. Except this day was different. The farmer knew the train schedule so at a certain time every day he would put his bull out to pasture using the daily schedule of the train. Only today our train was 30 minutes late due to the emergency cord problem. The farmer didn't know that we were not on schedule and according to his watch, it was safe to put his bull out to graze.

This crash created a big problem not only to the farmer but also to us. Picking up and carrying all your luggage and souvenirs to the next village was not an easy chore. Everyone was in the same situation so no one was able to help anyone else. The only way I could manage was to carry one suitcase 75 yards or so, sit it down, then go back and pick up the other suitcase along with a box of crystal wine glasses and move them past my first piece of luggage for another 75 yards. This way I could keep track of my things. As we passed the engine of the train, we could see the big bull wedged beneath. Everyone was exhausted when we arrived at the station. We had to wait there until they sent a train from Sophia to rescue all of us. Then at Sophia we caught another train to Belgrade, our original destination. This day was my birthday, and I must admit I have never spent such a miserable time. When we did get to Belgrade, there was nothing to do but collapse.

For the next 4 days, we had lots of sightseeing. Belgrade sits on the juncture of the Sava and the Danube Rivers. It used to be located in Yugoslavia, but today it is located in Serbia. Many of the buildings there are modern since this city received a lot of destruction from the wars. Belgrade Fortress is the most popular place for tourists and natives as well. Dating back from the first Celtic settlements, Belgrade Fortress has been constantly upgraded. From the fortress, there is a beautiful view overlooking the juncture of the two rivers. During our stay we also visited the bohemian quarter and the old palace. I bought three metal decorative plates that are hanging on my great wall today. One day we went to the American Club at the American Embassy for lunch. One evening we went to the theatre to see KOLO—the Yugoslav National Ballet.

August 22-25. Our train to Prague, Czechoslovakia, had three classes. Since we had no reservations, we were put into the bottom class with 6 people per compartment. Our cabin window was broken and wouldn't go down. We spent 18 hours on the train, and at night when we were sleeping, the controller kept waking us up and asking us to show our passports.

There was a lot to see in Prague. I especially liked St. Vitus Cathedral. It's an excellent example of gothic architecture, and it is located within the Prague Castle complex. The inside is a treasure trove of ornate tombs, sculptures, Czech Crown Jewels, and beautiful stained glass, especially the Mucha window.

Charles Bridge with its Baroque statues is another place for tourists, but it can be very crowded, and you have to watch your purse. A visit to the old Jewish Quarter and the Jewish Cemetery was interesting. At the town hall we saw a wedding in progress. We visited St. Nicholas Church, a Baroque church, on the Old Town Square. We spent one of our days visiting Karlstejn Castle which is about an hour's ride from Prague. It's a 14th century castle that was built to house the crown jewels of the Holy Roman Empire. There is a great view of the Moldau River from the castle. One evening we got tickets to *Laterna Magika* which had been introduced at the 1958 Brussels World's Fair and also at Expo 67 in Montreal. It's a kind of nonverbal play, circus, and ballet all combined in film. Everything seems expensive in Prague. Chocolate is especially expensive. One detail I especially remember about our stay in Prague was that there was never any hot water for our showers.

August 26-28. We got another train ride, this time a 22-hour train ride to Paris where we spent the next two days in a Youth Hostel. We got to see the usual tourist spots including the Sacre Coeur. At Notre Dame I climbed all the steps in the towers to the roof to photograph the chimère, those grotesque creatures which stand guard over the gargoyles. I got tickets to go to the top of the Eiffel Tower but had to wait in line an hour in order to get to the top level. It costs 2 F to the first level, 5 F to the second level, and 8 F to visit the top level. They take groups of 35 up to the top. In the evening I got a tickets to see *Oh Calcutta*. The theatre was small, but I had an excellent seat. On our last night in Paris, our leader had promised us a champagne party. Also he promised us that he would pay the airport tax for us. However our hostel did not permit alcohol so our going-away party got cancelled. Then when we got to the airport, we noticed that our airport tax had already been included. We decided that our leader missed his calling. He should have been a politician.

In the afternoon of the 28th we boarded our TWA 707, flight #8279, at Orly going to New York and then St. Louis where I would transfer for my flight to Cincinnati. We were warned about the turbulent weather at New York due to a hurricane. We landed at N.Y. At customs, they did not look into my suitcases, but they tore my purse apart, looking into all the pockets and crevices. After customs, we reboarded our flight to St. Louis. But I had just missed my TWA flight to Cincinnati so Allegany accepted my TWA ticket and sent me to Indianapolis. Then I eventually got another flight to Cincinnati. All's well that ends well.

Chapter Eleven

1973-1992 French and Russian Club Trips

After many trips abroad, I decided to share my travel experience with my foreign language students. Since French was my first foreign language that I taught, I thought that it would be a good idea to take my French students to France. I chose the tour company FACETS which featured French-American student travel. Since this was my first student trip abroad, I had many students who wanted to go. Along with another French teacher, we accumulated 28 students who wanted to go to France with us during the Christmas vacation. We departed Cincinnati December 26, 1973, on American Airlines Flight AA395 from Cincinnati to LaGuardia. Then we had a bus ride over to JFK. There we were put on Air France Flight 070 from NYC to Orly, Paris.

Before leaving, the other French teacher and I met with both parents and students. We laid out the itinerary which would include a guided visit of the city of Paris, plus Ile de la Cité, Notre Dame, la Sainte Chapelle, la Conciergerie, Chartres, Château de Rambouillet, the Eiffel Tower, Jeu de Paume Museum, the Louvre, Versailles and Malmaison. We had some general rules of conduct such as no guys in any girls' rooms at any time and no wandering off without one of us. On later student trips, the rules would be expanded.

Our only unpleasant experience was that we were in France on New Year's Eve with nothing to do. I tried to find some kind of student party, but everything was booked-up. As a last resort I took the students out on the Champs-Elysées to ring in the New Year. That was not a good decision. It was very similar to being on Times Square to ring in the New Year. I could not have imagined the wild antics of the Frenchmen. I was lucky to get back to the hotel with all of the students intact. The French were trying to hug and kiss my girl students. As a last resort I had all the girls link arms around a large tree and kick anyone who tried to reach us. I looked for help to one of the nearby gendarmes. And his answer was, "What did you expect on New Year's Eve on the Champs-Elysées?" I know what I didn't expect—local chaos. That is a New Year's Eve that I will never forget, and I am sure that the 28 students will always remember it as well.

We returned to the U.S. on January 3, 1974, from Orly Airport on Air France Flight #077 to JFK, than a transfer to LaGuardia where we departed on American Flight #584 to Cincinnati.

In the following years I would take 20 plus student trips to France. The plan was usually the same. I would choose a trip to France proper, or France and a surrounding country such as France and Germany, France and England, or France and Switzerland. I would announce to my students that a trip to France was planned for the spring break which usually lasted about 10 days. Sometime in October or November I would hold a meeting in my classroom in the evening for both students and parents and would pass out an itinerary and a list of my rules for discussion.

A typical French Trip would usually coincide with Fairfield's Spring Break. We usually had 10 days, and it was easy to find student trips to Europe for that time frame. We would usually fly into Paris for 2-3 days. During that time I would always show my students what I wanted them to see—the Unicorn Tapestries at Cluny Museum, Venus de Milo and the Mona Lisa at the Louvre, Notre Dame with its bells, gargoyles, and stained glass, Napoleon's Tomb at Les Invalides, the Sacre Coeur, the view from the top of Montmartre, the bookstalls along the Seine where they could buy Parisian prints and books, and the beautiful stained glass windows of the Sainte Chapelle. The Sainte Chapelle is frequently missed by most of the tours.

If time allowed when we visited Notre Dame, we would climb the steps to the top of the towers where they could see the large bell and have their photo taken with their favorite grotesque chimère. I always included a boat ride on the Seine either in the afternoon or in the evening, and a walk down the Champs-Elysées. They could see the Eiffel Tower from almost any vantage point in Paris, but with so little time, we could not spend half a day waiting in line to go up.

On day four we would leave Paris and head towards the châteaux country stopping to see Azay-le-Rideau, Chenonceaux, and a picture stop at Chambord. Then we would head west to climb to the top of Mont St. Michel. Turning southward we would travel through some of the wine country to Carcassonne and Lourdes, then on to Nice and the French Rivera before heading back to Paris and home. If time allowed there might have been a visit to Versailles.

In the spring of 1975 I took some of my Russian students and two adults to the Soviet Union. I felt comfortable doing this since Big Brother was watching everything. For example, there was little or no crime at this time because there were police and "snitches" everywhere. The Russian people felt obliged to turn you in if you made up your own rules. Our group was handled by Intourist, and there were no problems since I had told my students what to expect. For example, do not try to sell your blue jeans when asked by the Russians to do so. Blue jeans were a hot item in the Soviet Union at this time because there were none at their department stores. Do not exchange money with the Russians when asked to do so. Exchange money only at the banks. Photos are allowed, but be aware of buildings in the background. You may want a picture of a statue or a picturesque building, but you may be stopped because there may be something behind the statue or building that the Russians don't want photographed. The hotels had a table with a woman in charge who monitored everything that happened on her floor. If you left your room, you had to turn your key into her instead of the main desk.

One interesting fact I had told my students in advance. "Watch your step" when going up or down steps because they were not all the same height. Also when getting into or out of the elevators, pay attention to the level of the floor where the doors open. Even with my warnings, I found my students stumbling into and out of the elevators and the rooms. We all joked and kidded one another each time that this happened. Even with the warning, we were always caught off guard.

147

There was another interesting fact that was different. When going to a play, opera, or ballet, you ate dinner after the entertainment, not before. This meant that dinner at the hotel or restaurant began usually at 10:00 P.M. This was a little extreme even by European standards. Dinner in France or Spain usually begins at 7:00 or 8:00 P.M. No one eats at 5:00 P.M. as in the U.S. Also it is possible that you may encounter a waitress that refuses to serve you because you are an American. She contends that she is only doing her duty in refusing to serve the enemy.

Our trip from New York via Finnair landed in Helsinki where we had a sightseeing trip including The American Embassy, the Cathedral, and Sibellius Monument. In the evening we went to the train station and boarded a train to Leningrad. Surrounding the train station were lots of drunks lying around. One of them kicked me as I went past. We had snacks on the train because there was no dining car. The train made several stops during the night for passport control. The next morning we arrived in Leningrad and our Intourist Guide, Lydia, was waiting for us.

We checked in at the October Hotel and were assigned our rooms before beginning our morning sightseeing tour of the city. Then we had lunch at the Sadko Restaurant. For the afternoon sightseeing tour, we were to meet in the hotel lobby. While waiting in the lobby, I decided that I needed another roll of film which was in my room. I asked one of my male students to watch my purse for me while I ran back to my room. Minutes later I returned to the lobby, and in the center of the lobby was my purse sitting all by itself with no one watching it. I picked it up quickly since it contained all the passports for my group plus all my money. I boarded the bus which was waiting for us, and when I saw my student, I asked him why he abandoned my purse. He replied that he didn't want to miss the bus. I guess he thought the bus would leave without me. Thinking back, I guess my purse was safe because Big Brother was everywhere, but that didn't explain my student's actions. In today's society you couldn't sit any size purse down in a hotel lobby and expect to ever see it again.

The rest of our afternoon was spent at the Hermitage Museum. In the evening after dinner, Lydia took us for a tour of the subway stations. The Russians are very proud of their subway stations. Many of them are decorated like palaces with crystal chandeliers. The one I liked best was the Pushkin Station.

I called Natasha when I returned to the hotel. She was the one person that I had met in 1971 while I was studying at Leningrad. We had corresponded several times by mail after I had returned home. She was an English and Russian teacher so we had many things in common. She wanted to show me her apartment so we made arrangements to meet the following evening. She lived there with her husband who was crippled from a swimming accident. I had no worries about leaving my students at the hotel since Big Brother was watching them. I had brought several gifts from the U.S. to give her, and she gave me several books, items that we could use in our language classes. Natasha picked me up at the hotel in a car, and we drove to her apartment in the outskirts of Leningrad. She had prepared a roast duck for dinner.

We had a great time sharing stories about our lives. At 12:30 A.M. I told Natasha that it was time for me to return to the hotel. Of course, I was thinking that she was going to drive me back to the hotel. But instead she gave me directions on how to return. It seems that she had borrowed the car from one of her friends, and she no longer had access to it. Her directions were as follows: "When exiting the apartment building, follow the dark lane to the main highway. Stand on the main highway until a truck comes by, then put your hand out as a hitchhiker would and hail the truck, and beg a ride back to Leningrad."

I was in shock. I had only hitchhiked once before in 1968 in Africa with two other girls in the daytime. And that was of my own choosing. Now I was walking down a dark lane, standing out on a dark highway, begging a ride back to my hotel after midnight. I had done some scary things in my life, but this one was at the top of the list. Natasha explained that this was very common in Leningrad. Truck drivers would pick up pedestrians and deliver them to their destinations in return for some rubles. It was very dark on the highway, and Natasha did not accompany me. Eventually a truck came by so I stuck my thumb out, and it stopped. I told him the name of my hotel in Russian and he took me there. I was so happy to get back to my room. I felt that the least Natasha could have done was to accompany me back to the highway and wait until I found a truck for transportation. I was used to experiencing foreign customs, but this one put me into shock. However, after that episode I never corresponded with Natasha again. I am sure she never realized why, but I could never forget the frightening experience that she had put me through.

Chapter Twelve

1982 Other Language Club Trips

Once in a while I would take some of the German or Spanish students on a spring break trip. There would usually be about 7-8 students and maybe 1-2 adults. The adults might be the parents of some of the students, but not necessarily. They tended to be friends or acquaintances of mine who knew about my trips. The students were all German or Spanish students at my high school and would have to be in good standing with their foreign language teachers. I did not want to get myself into a bad situation out of the country. On April 4, 1982, I took some German students to the German speaking countries. We left on TWA Flight #424 from Cincinnati to Kennedy, and then caught a Lufthansa Flight #409 to Munich. The tour company always puts several schools together in order to make it feasible to continue offering student trips. So my group of 8 along with the German students from 3 other high schools totaled 50, and our bus only held 49. So three of the smaller students had to squeeze together. Our first stop was Salzburg where we spent the night.

The next morning we toured the Hohensalzburg Fortress, then left for the city of Melk, Austria, where we had lunch at the beautiful Benedictine Abbey, then on to Vienna. After dinner we went to the Kursalon located in the city park for performances of the various waltzes. Later we had a ride on the once-around Ferris wheel. The next morning we toured Schöbrunn Palace, the former summer residence of the Habsburgs. Schöbrunn Palace was built to outshine Versailles. Then we went to the Lipizzans Winter Riding School to see the horses perform. More sightseeing took us to Belvedere Palace and Gardens, then to St. Stephen's Church. In the evening after dinner, the group went to Grinzing for the wine stube.

We left early the next morning for a long drive. We retraced our steps back to Salzburg and Melk, then on to Innsbruck where we checked in to the Hotel Bellevue which sits high in the mountains with a good view of the city. In the evening after dinner there was a typical Tyrolean Evening with lots of yodeling and a woodcutters' dance. The next morning we drove to Vaduz, Lichtenstein, where we had lunch and shopping, then a 2-hour drive on to Lucerne. We had great rooms in the Flora Hotel which is near the Old Gate Tower. In the evening we had a Swiss Fondue Party in the old part of the city. It included lots of Swiss flag throwing.

The next morning included lots of shopping in Lucerne before we left for Zurich. En route we passed Lake Constance, Bregenz, and Lindau before stopping at Fussen to see the castle. Next we stopped in Oberammergau where the Heigl Shop opened its doors for us to shop. Then we were off to Munich where our driver Ralph left us. The next day we did all the city sightseeing. Later we took a trip to Dachau which included a tour plus a film, and a trip through the museum. That evening we went to the Hofbrauhaus for beer and singing. We left the next morning for our trip home. The check-in at Lufthansa was terrible. They had our seats all scrambled up. There were not enough seats in the non-smoking area. Finally they threw 50 seats at us and told us to work it out ourselves. We did just that. Our flight took us to Dusseldorf then on to N.Y. and home.

In the spring of 1983 I took another group to the German speaking countries. We departed the Cincinnati airport on March 31 on TWA Flight #424. We arrived N.Y. and took the shuttle bus to the Pan Am Building where we caught PA Flight #72 on a 747 to Frankfurt, Germany. The plane held 389 passengers with 1 empty seat. The flight lasted 7 hours and as usual we landed in the A.M. Fred was our guide. We checked into our Novotel which is part of a French chain.

The next morning we took the Romantic Road to Munich via Rothenberg with stops along the way for meals and shopping. In Munich everyone wanted to visit the Hofbrauhaus so we did. The following morning we visited the Olympic Village, and Nymphenburg Palace where the Bavarian rulers used to live. Then we made a stop at the Marienplatz in the heart of the city for the 11:00 A.M. daily performance of the Glockenspeil. Then we lunched at the Marienplatz Square plus we shopped for beer steins. The next morning we drove to Salzburg where we visited the old castle at the top of the hill. We had a photo stop at the beautiful Mirabelle Palace and Gardens.

We had lunch in Salzburg and then a drive into Innsbruck via Berchtesgaden. We had dinner in Innsbruck. Later that evening we walked to the Golden Roof in the old city. The next day we drove from Innsbruck to Mitterwald, Garmish, then to Oberammergau, site of the Passion Play, then on to Fussen where we visited the castle and had lunch. Then we drove to Vaduz, Liechtenstein. We said, "Hello", to the Baron and then drove on to Lucerne where we stayed. That evening we took a walk to see the famous Lion of Lucerne. We had two nights in Lucerne. The second night we went to a Swiss Folklore Event at the Chalet along the lakefront.

The next morning we left Lucerne and drove to Zurich, the Rhein Falls, and the Black Forrest. We visited the castle at Heidelburg before going to Mannheim and Frankfurt for our trip home. One of the boys had bought 3 beer steins for his friends back home. When we arrived in N.Y. there was so much confusion going through passport control and customs, then hurrying for our flight home, that the boy with the beer steins set his package down and forgot them. That sent the airport into a frenzy—a large unattended package with no owner in sight and no name on the package. Once you clear customs, you are not allowed to return. That was a big mix-up which sent security into chaos about what to do. I explained to those in control, but they would not release the package at that time. Later when everything was cleared up, the beer steins were returned to the boy via the post office. Today I don't think that they would return the package. I think they probably would put it into a canister and blow it up.

Chapter Thirteen

1982 On My Own

I did have another amusing experience. In the spring of 1982 while traveling with my students, I noticed several shops which had Ferrandiz woodcarvings in the windows. Being on tour I could not stop and investigate. Then in Switzerland, I found a Ferrandiz figurine to add to my collection. It was an older one, no longer being made. I said to myself, "Surely there are more older figurines sitting on the shelves of some small store." The Ferrandiz Factory is located in Val Gardena, Italy. So in the summer of 1982 I decided to rent a car and drive by myself through Germany, Switzerland, northern Italy, and eastern France. Perhaps I could find more of the old Ferrandiz woodcarvings.

The artist Juan Ferrandiz was alive at that time and still producing his wooden hand-painted figurines. A distinctive thing about his figurines is that they are hand-carved in Alpine Maple with some little bunny, squirrel, or sheep along side of the main figure. His figurines were expensive $200.00 for the 6" one and $100.00 for the 3" figure. But it was worth it if I could find an older one, no longer in production.

I landed in Frankfurt, Germany, and that's where I got my red Ford Fiesta car. A man met me in the lower level of the airport and gave me the keys along with the directions. But he spoke no English. When I pulled out on the Autobahn, it was raining hard, and I didn't know where the wipers were. Learning the ins and outs of a new car while entering Germany's super highway in a rainstorm is not a pleasant way to begin a trip.

I had made out my own schedule of cities that I wanted to visit: Coburg, Rothenburg, Munich, Oberammergau, Innsbruck, Ravensburg, Zurich, Lucerne, Berne, Basel, Strasbourg, Freiburg, and Heidelburg. I would spend one night in each city. I thought about Val Gardena, but when I got to the Italian border there was a lot of talk about highway bandits in Italy so I chose not to go there.

Parking in Germany is not the same as that in the U.S. I would drive around until late afternoon when I saw a hotel. However, the parking was not nearby. One has to use the Park Platz in the larger cities. So when you found a place to park, you might have lost the hotel. In a smaller city you could find a motel with a parking lot. I spent two weeks looking for older Ferrandiz figurines, but with no success. Also being on my own, I got the least bit discombobulated.

I frequently lost my scarf, my gloves, my map, or my sunglasses, even my reading glasses which were on a cord around my neck. Sometimes I even had difficulty in finding my car. I had a little tape recorder with me, and as I strolled along the streets looking in the shop windows, I would talk into my tape recorder making note of buildings that I passed or landmarks that I passed so that I could find my way back to my car. The streets in Europe are not divided into blocks like they are in the U.S. So if I wanted to see my car again, I had to make a recording of streets and buildings that I had seen.

The main difference between this trip and all the others is that on this trip I was lonely. On all the other trips, I traveled alone, but I was always part of a group so I was never really alone. Now when I went for breakfast, I found myself envious of all the groups talking and socializing. I was lonely, with no one to talk to for 2 weeks. During all my previous travels, I had never realized how much fun it was to travel with a group. Now I had no one to share my thoughts and possible frustrations with.

One day in Oberammergau, Germany, famous for its Passion Play which happens every ten years, I had walked through most of the small city stores when I noticed that my glasses were no longer hanging around my neck. So I retraced my steps asking if anyone found a pair of grasses. No one had, but one shopkeeper gave me back my scarf which I had left in his store. Finally I had given up the search when I had to stop for a red light. I looked in the gutter, and there were my glasses unbroken just lying there waiting for me to claim them. What are the odds of finding your glasses at your feet when you have given up looking for them?

I did have a few problems driving on my own. No one told me that I had to let the car warm up. I only found this out after it stalled in the middle of an intersection. Fortunately for me two young Germans came to my rescue. They pushed me out of the way, and I could start the car again. Also I always had problems with the hand brake. I frequently had to park on an incline so I had to use the hand brake. When it came time to leave, I did not have enough strength in my hands to release the brake. Once again I had to rely on the help of some gentleman. The worst problem, however, was driving, shifting gears, looking for street signs, watching for traffic, searching for souvenir shops, all while trying to read a map. The one thing that I frequently overlooked was the sign indicating a one-way street. I frequently found myself driving the wrong way down a one-way street.

One city that I really wanted to visit was Munich, and I really had a hard time finding the center of the town. I kept driving and driving ignoring the sign that said "Centrum". Finally in total frustration, I saw a Munich taxi, and from the front seat of my car, I hired a taxi to lead me to the Hofbräuhaus in downtown Munich. From there I knew that I could find the nearby Platzl Hotel. I had stayed there before on a former trip with students. I distinctly remember taking the students to the Hofbräuhaus and leaving them for a half hour while I got a table next door at a café and relaxed with a glass of wine while waiting for them. This way I could avoid all the noise in the Hofbräuhaus and collect my thoughts.

At the end of two weeks, I knew that I had wasted my time looking for any older figurines. At the trip's end, I took the Autobahn north back to Frankfort where I had to deliver the car. En route, I decided to stop at Heidelburg, a small city perched on the hill. There I did find one older Ferrandiz figurine, but that was an expensive trip for just one figurine. Now I was sailing along on the Autobahn, and I turned on the radio because I was near an American base. Up to this point I had been unable to get any international news in English. The announcer on the radio said, "Now about the air controllers strike in the U.S." I was really upset since now

I would be stuck in Frankfurt until Reagan lifted the strike. I was lucky however because I only got stranded for one day. However, that could have been very expensive for me had the strike lasted a week or two. Frankfurt is a very expensive airport, and during the strike no planes were allowed to leave since they could not land in the U.S.

Chapter Fourteen

MIle's Rules and Regulations

Here is a list of personal rules and regulations that I required of all students. They were called Mademoiselle's Rules or MIle's Rules

They are:

1. Curfew—A general curfew of 11:00 P.M. or 12:00 midnight will be in effect at all times. Your parents will decide which of the two curfews they prefer. At that time you must be inside your hotel room unless you are with me or have my permission to be somewhere else. I will make a bed check every night, and you may not leave your room after I have made my rounds. If you are not in your room when I check it, you must stop in my room and let me know that you are in. Do not send me word that you are in. I must see you in person. I will not retire for the evening until everyone is in. Please have a little consideration for me. I need my sleep, as all of you will, so please let me go to bed at 12:30. Staying up late at night only leads to oversleeping in the morning. Also there is to be no shouting or screaming in the hotels at any time. After 10:00 P.M. strict silence must be observed.

2. You are expected to take two meals with the group: breakfast and dinner. These are important times

for announcements and changes. Also you are expected to be on all the tours. If you are feeling sick and need to stay at the hotel, then you need to see me concerning a meal. For lunch you will probably be on your own so you may eat with whomever and whererver you please.

3. Boys are not allowed in the rooms of the girls, nor are girls allowed in the rooms of the boys, unless I am present in the room.

4. Alcohol—With your afternoon and evening meal and IN MY PRESENCE, you may SAMPLE a limited amount of beer or wine provided that your parents have signed the permission slip prior to departure. Alcoholic beverages must NEVER be taken to your room for consumption. If you haven't finished your bottle of wine at the dinner table, that's too bad since you must leave it there. Hard liquor is strictly forbidden at any time. I will strongly enforce this rule—Don't spoil the day for you or me or others.

5. Motor vehicles—Student tour companies do not permit students to rent cars, motor vehicles, motor scooters, or motorbikes in Europe.

6. Drugs, knives, fireworks are out. If such items are found in your possession, you'll be sent directly home at your parents' expense. You will not pass Go, and you will not collect $200.00.

7. Many people on the continent speak little or no English. For this reason, you should know a few simple expressions in French: hello, thank you, good-bye, please, etc. However, many waiters, shopkeepers,

bus drivers, etc. do speak English and want to practice their English. Don't be upset if, when you are speaking French to a waiter, he answers you in English. He has detected your accent, and perhaps he wants to show off his English. He is not saying that he doesn't understand your French. In confirming an order, he may trust his English more that he trusts your French. Just take this in your stride, and don't make a federal case out of it. You will have ample opportunity to speak and use your French.

8. Picking up towels, ashtrays, and mugs, as souvenirs in the U.S. may have become an accepted practice. However, in Europe waiters and maids are themselves required to pay for anything that is missing. Under no circumstances should you take away any inappropriate souvenirs. That is stealing.

9. Occasionally a hotel room in Europe comes equipped with a fully-stocked refrigerated mini bar. Should you have such a mini bar in your room, under no circumstances should you consume any alcoholic beverages from the mini bar, since it is against my rules to drink in your room in the first place. In the second place, you may only drink in my presence. This means that you must invite me to your room, and I am sure that you won't want to do that. I will try to remove any bar keys before I issue you your room key, but in case I slip up, please turn the bar key in to me or the front desk.

NOTE: items including bottled water or coca-cola in the mini bar are extremely expensive. This is just another reason why not to use the mini bar. Please realize that, besides water, any drinks that you order with your meal or separately are to be paid for by you. Nothing is free or almost nothing. No drinks, except water, are included with your meal. Should the waiter ask you if you want something to drink, he is really asking you if you want to purchase a drink? Don't be afraid to ask him the price of a coca-cola or a glass of wine. Afterwards, the waiter will give you a check that will say "service compris" or "service non-compris". "Serivce compris" means that the tip is included. "Service non-compris," means that a tip, "pourboire", is expected. If the waiter asks for your room number, please advise him that you want to pay for the drink now. Otherwise, a room tab will be applied, and paying hotel tabs at checkout will hold up the tour departure. Drinks at breakfast, however, are included: that is coffee, tea, or hot chocolate. Orange juice can be ordered, but it is not included in the continental breakfast and must be paid for separately.

10. Please watch your personal items carefully such as passport, camera, traveler's checks, wallet, and other important items. Do not leave these items scattered around your hotel room. Try to keep them on your person or perhaps locked in your suitcase. If you are going to lock your suitcase for any reason at any time during the trip, I must be given a duplicate key prior

to departure. Do not give it to me on the plane going over. Give me the key several days prior to departure so that I will have time to tag it. Much of the time I will have your passport, but you must be responsible for it when it is in your possession. You will need your passport every time you exchange money at the bank or at the exchange, at border crossings, and at customs. *Do not store your passport in your suitcase.* It is your ID, and you may never know when it needs to be shown so keep it with you. You must also be responsible for your money. I will keep your plane tickets until needed.

11. Do not change rooms after I have assigned them. If, for some reason, you can't get along with your roommate, I will try to solve the problem. I must know where you are sleeping so that the evening room check goes smoothly.

12. Bus Etiquette—Please be courteous and listen to the explanations of the guides and courier. This means not only on the bus but also in the museums. Try to refrain from chatting on the bus and in the museums when the guide is explaining the important facts and sights.

13. No smoking on the bus or anywhere near me. (Please)

In retrospect, the only addition I would make to the above rules is to ask the students to sign an agreement that he or she would abide by these rules.

Chapter Fifteen

Mlle's Trip Procedures

Following is a list of trip procedures that I made for the trip to France and Switzerland, but they would be adjusted for any of the other student trips. The prices quoted were in effect in 1978.

1. Put your initials on the outside of your suitcase using colored tape with large letters.
2. Take a travel alarm for every two people.
3. Take hot chocolate, coffee, or instant tea, if you want. However you will need to purchase a portable instant heating element for heating water in the cup. You will also need a very heavy plastic or glass cup in which to prepare the coffee, tea, or hot chocolate. The dual voltage-heating element sells for $12.95 at Bankhardt's. Any electric appliance that you intend to use on the trip will need to be used with an adapter or converter or both. Both items can be purchased at Bankhardt's (Downtown Cincinnati or Forest Fair). A converter is for use in changing the electrical current from the 110 use in the U.S. to the 220 use in Europe. Bankhardt's has a converter for use for 50 watts to 1600 watts ($18.00). They also have a set of 5 adapter plugs for $9.00. The converter and adapter sets are available at $23.50 for 50 watts to 1600 watts. If your

appliance has a built in converter, all you need is the set of adapter plugs. If your portable heating element does not specify European use, you will need to plug it into a converter + adapter. Perhaps several of you could go together for purchase of one or both of the above. Buy them as soon as possible.

4. Take along an ample supply of lifesavers, hard candy, and snacks, snacks, and snacks. As you eat the snacks, you will make room for all the purchases that you will want to make. If you must chew gum, please do so without a lot of snapping, popping, and cracking in order to cut down on the wear and tear of my nervous system.

5. Watch your luggage allowance. The limit is 44 lbs. including the large suitcase and your flight bag. You must get all your personal belongings into these two items. You may NOT take any other luggage, however you are allowed to take a separate camera case, and the girls are allowed a reasonably-sized purse. My suggestion is not to exceed 38-40 lbs. going over. This will allow you a margin for the return trip. If you are not content with the flight bag that the tour company supplied, you may want to investigate another type. However, please remember that the flight bag should be capable of being placed beneath the seat in front of you on the plane. Also you will be responsible for carrying your flight bag at all times as it will NOT be checked through with the large suitcase.

6. Make sure that you have a comfortable pair of walking shoes. Do NOT take along new shoes with the idea of breaking them in while in Europe. Make sure that they have already been broken in. Take along a few band-aids for cuts and blisters.

7. Put all toilet articles in plastic containers. Glass is both heavy and breakable. Take only an 11-day supply of toothpaste, hair spray, deodorant, make-up, etc.

8. When we go to France and Switzerland, you will have to learn the value of both the French franc and the Swiss franc. The names are the same, but the values are different. The French franc is currently worth about 21¢. You will get about 4.9893 French francs for one American dollar. At present the Swiss franc is worth 77¢ so you would get 1.3054 Swiss francs for an American dollar. This is subject to change daily. The American dollar right now is weak. A small calculator might be helpful when making purchases. Also a currency calculator would be helpful. Take along $20 to $25 in single dollar bills to be kept for the end of the trip. They will be valuable when we get ready to leave France or Switzerland. Do not spend them until necessary. You may also find a need for a $5.00 bill. The rest of your money should be in $10.00 or $20.00 traveler's checks. Do not purchase $50.00 traveler's checks. Instead, buy the 10's or 20's. Almost any make of traveler's checks is acceptable. Don't forget to deposit $50.00 with me by mid-March for use in an emergency fund. I must have

the money early enough to buy traveler's checks. I do not want to carry the emergency money in cash. Any unspent emergency money that you do not need will be returned to you upon return. Take along ample reading material (book, magazine, etc.) You will have to wait several hours at airports depending on our flights plus a 9-hour plane ride, plus the plane trip home.

9. There will usually be 3 students to a room. Adults will be housed two to a room. I will make every effort to keep those traveling together in the same room; however, please realize that every hotel does not exactly fit our individual needs. From time to time I may have to ask you to room temporarily with some other tour participant. Please try to co-operate in this matter. I will try my best to accommodate you, but at times my hands may be tied. There are also times when you may want to change roommates because you have met someone new and prefer that person to your original roommate. I will still try to accommodate you in this instance. After all, part of the value of the trip is in making new friends. Remember you cannot change roommates without my permission.

10. Be prepared to find new and different customs. Try to avoid the idea of "That's stupid" simply because they differ from our own customs. After all is said and done, you have spent a lot of money to explore different cultures so don't expect to find an exact replica of the U.S. when you are in France or Switzerland. If we are

just seeing a "little America", then you have wasted your money.

11. You may want to take along several 19¢ stamps to use at Kennedy Airport. While waiting for our international flight, you may want to send a postcard to friends and family at home. However, after leaving the U.S., your American postage stamps are not valid. In France and Switzerland, you will have to purchase foreign postage stamps if you want to send postcards or letters home. If you have lots of friends to write, you may want to buy the Avery self-adhesive unprinted labels, available at most office supply stores 200/$5.00. These could be typed in advance of the trip. Then when writing home, you will save valuable time in addressing the post cards. With the pre-addressed labels, just pull them off, buy a stamp, jot down a few words, and mail. These labels are 1"X 3". If you don't use the labels, bring along the U.S. addresses that you need.

12. Bring along a small bar of soap for bathing and washing out things. Soap will probably be furnished everywhere, but you may find that it lathers differently. Also a washcloth and an older towel might come in handy. If your suitcase if crowded for the return trip, you can leave them.

13. Your trip will be best remembered if you decide to keep a diary. Get a small one or convert a small notebook into a diary. The notebook and diary can also be used for a record of all pictures taken. In addition, it will be useful to write down all purchases

169

and their equivalent prices. This will help you when going through customs. The notebook can also be used for useful information given by the tour guide such as the history of the monuments, the exhibits at the museum, and the times for the next day's meals. All your thoughts will be enjoyable to read in years hence.

14. Take along an adequate supply of film. Firm is more expensive abroad, and it is not always available. For a first trip abroad it is quite possible to take 200 pictures. Often students bring 3 rolls of film and shoot one of these before arriving in Europe. Do not bring along the mailers. Put all film in your flight bag and keep it there throughout the trip. It is safer there. Always carry one or two extra rolls of film with you in purse or pocket. If not, you may run out of film during the visit of a tourist site.

15. Take along a small bottle of Murine or other eye wash and keep it with you on the plane in your purse or flight bag. You will find the eye drops useful after the overnight flight to Paris and the one returning home. Also very useful on the plane are footlets. This way you can remove your shoes and still have something to keep your feet warm. They also should be in your flight bag.

16. If you intend to listen to the stereo music plus the movie, take along $8.00 to rent the earphones ($4.00 each way). The movie probably will not be a great one, but it will give you something to do for 2 hours.

If we are fortunate enough to get a Delta flight, the earphones are free.

17. If you intend to do any light laundry, buy a set of plastic clothespins with a hanger attached. This will allow you to hang up any light articles that you have hand-washed.

18. You will probably have toilet facilities in your room; however a robe might come in handy for use in the hall. Light slippers and a pair of thongs for use in the shower are recommended. Girls might also need a shower cap.

19. An optimistic view would be to take along a pair of sunglasses especially if your eyes are sun-sensitive.

20. Sometime soon you will want to get some guidebooks on France and Switzerland plus some maps of the area. One good guidebook is Baedeker's France or Baedeker's Switzerland. They cost $22.95 each and come equipped with road maps. They are well worth the money. Plus they can be shared with one another. Also helpful are the green Michelin Guides for France ($14.95) and for Switzerland also ($14.95). All of the above books plus many others are available at the local bookstores.

21. Now is a good time to check out books on the history of France and Switzerland from your local library. The more reading that you do in advance, the better prepared you will be when you arrive. I highly recommend extensive reading prior to the trip. Know what you are going to see before you get there.

22. I also recommend taking along a small pocket French language dictionary if you have had some training in French. Otherwise, a dictionary is not needed.

23. We will have a telephone chain. I will give you a list of all phone numbers of the participants on the trip. In case of an extended delay leaving the departure city, I will telephone my mother, Mrs. Kuhn, who will be the first one on the list. She, then, will relay all necessary information to the second person on the list, who will call the third person, etc. That way if we should be delayed in Europe or even New York, everyone's family would be advised of the change. If for some reason, the family to be called next cannot be reached, skip the name temporarily and phone the next family on the list. Then later, try to locate the name that you skipped and give them the needed information. This system hopefully will prevent all the families from arriving at the Cinti airport and finding none of us there.

24. IMPORTANT: PLEASE LEAVE THIS TELEPHONE LIST CLOSE TO THE PHONE AT HOME AND ADVISE EVERYONE AT HOME WHAT TO DO TO ACTIVATE IT. It will save a lot of problems.

25. Souvenirs: The best souvenirs to bring back should be watercolor prints, head scarves (both silk and nylon), perfume, watches, and music boxes. You will also find a lot of knick-knacks. Some of them are quite heavy so watch your weight allowance. Most items are best bought at local stores rather than at the airport. You will see a lot of attractive prints that can be brought

home. They will roll up and can fit into the corner or top of your suitcase. Then they can be framed at home. Keep a list of all souvenirs purchased and prices paid for use at customs.

26. A small travel umbrella or rain hat or both may be of great value. Both items can be purchased abroad, but you may have to wait until we have free time.

27. Make sure that the coat that you wear over is heavy enough. One with a zip-out lining would be ideal. The best type is a coat that functions as a raincoat.

28. Under no circumstances should you promise Mother, Dad, Grandmother, etc. that you will call them when you arrive abroad. This only leads to a lot of lost time waiting for the call to go though. Plus a simple little delay could be thought of as a catastrophe to one who is pacing the floor waiting for the phone to ring. Let's function on the old adage that *"No news is good news"*. It really is not fair to the rest of the group to hold up a bus or tour while one person calls home.

29. One critical part of the trip is TIME. It is vital that you know when the plane is leaving, when the tour starts, when breakfast and dinner are being served, and when everything is happening. If you don't own a dependable watch, please borrow one for the trip, or purchase an inexpensive Timex before departure. One that you will buy in Lucerne at the end of the trip will not help you. The last thing that you should do before retiring in the evening is to find out what the following day's activities are and when. Check and double check everything. A good guess is NOT

acceptable. From time to time, you will get a rest or lunch break while traveling on the bus. The return time will be announced. Please, please be on time. If someone is late, let it NOT be you or anyone in my group. Getting lost is also not a valid excuse for being late. As you exit the bus, look around and get your bearings. Focus on one identifiable landmark, and above all, verify the return time. Every time the bus has to wait for one or two late people, everyone on the bus gets to see less than what he paid for. Please be considerate and be on time.

30. Take along a box of Puffs. They will come in handy if you happen to get a cold, and they will also double as toilet paper. The toilet paper in Europe falls short of our expectations. It is a constant topic of conversation. If you are the least bit picky about this, be prepared and bring along some tissues. The tissues can be squeezed into shoes and between items in the suitcase. Also carry some with you. While on the subject, be prepared to see toilets that do not resemble toilets, as we know them. They come in many sizes and shapes, and you may want to write a book about them when you return home.

31. As far as clothes go, the climate in France and Switzerland should be very similar to the climate here in April, so dress accordingly. I would definitely take a warm sweater for use under your coat or by itself. You ought to have one dress-up outfit for a visit to a disco, or a possible farewell party, or perhaps the Follies. Most of the time you may dress casually.

32. Something of value, but not essential, is a passport case, obtainable at Bankhardts. ($37.50-$50.00) It is extremely handy for keeping all the important papers—passport, traveler's checks, tickets, singles, etc. In addition to the passport case, everyone should have one or two change purses. I generally keep all my American change in a small coin purse so that I don't get it mixed up with the foreign currency. American coins cannot be used abroad, but you need to have some coins with you for use when you arrive back in the U.S. and also for use when exchanging money. So don't get rid of your American change before leaving the country, but do have a separate coin purse to put American money in. Try to find a coin purse divided into 3 parts—one for American money, one for French francs, and one for Swiss francs. You may also need a few dollars when we arrive in the U.S. so don't spend all your singles.

33. Take along a chap-stick for your lips.

34. It is usual in Europe to tip the tour conductor and the bus drive at the end of the trip. This is the only tip that is NOT covered by your tour price. Generally, every student contributes $20.00-$25.00 (Adults contribute $25.00-$30.00) at the end of the trip for a collection to be presented to the tour conductor and the driver separately. Please try to save this amount because it is needed at a time when you have the least amount of money. You may tap your Emergency Fund for all or part, if needed. I will collect the money from you personally and give it to the driver and to the tour

conductor on behalf of our group at the end of our tour. If you prefer, you may give me the tip money before leaving the U.S.

35. Every year someone manages to fall victim to one of the many pickpockets in Europe. We will be most vulnerable when on the Paris Metro and in the Louvre. I advise purchasing some kind of on-the-body belt where you can store your passport and money. The items below are available at Bankhardt's. Neck-Safe for passport and money ($9.50); Bra-Stash for ($4.75); Waist-Safe for PP ($10.00); Clip-safe for PP and $ ($10.25); Sock-Safe for ($9.50). There is also a variety of money belts on the market. Please find something similar to the above for your own protection, and remember, both passports and money are very much in demand.

36. I plan to purchase some French Francs and some Swiss Francs in this country prior to leaving. I recommend having some foreign currency on hand when you arrive in the country. Therefore, I will attach a list of currency options for you to consider. I will buy the foreign money for you. This would be in addition to your American singles and Traveller's Checks and Emergency Fund Money which you should have. Available will be $25.00 or $50.00 in French Francs plus $25.00 or $50.00 in Swiss Francs. You will have a choice of which to purchase, but I do feel that you should invest $50.00 to $100.00 in foreign currency before leaving the country. This will not be the very best rate of exchange, but it keeps us from spending

valuable time standing in lines abroad. If for some reason, you do not spend all that you purchased, it can be part of the tip going to the driver and the tour director at the trip's end. If the above directions do not answer all your questions, please ask me.

Chapter Sixteen

Problems With Students

I have had few problems with students without asking them to sign the Rules and Regulations Form, but there were a few instances when I threatened to send one of my students home. On student trips, my group of students would be joined with one or two other groups of high school students and their teacher. We would all be on the same bus, and we would all be in the same hotels during our trip. However each teacher would be in charge of his individual group, and the tour director had no control over our students. I as a teacher would act as a substitute parent for each of my students. However I did encounter a problem on one of my trips when one of my students was enamored with another French group that was on our bus. Their French teacher was much more lenient than I was. So one evening after an outing, my student "conveniently" got lost and went with the other group because they had fewer restrictions, and they could stay out as late as they pleased. The main doors to student hotels are usually locked at 11:00 P.M. and arrivals after that have to ring the bell in order to get the night watchman to let them in.

I had already made my nighttime bed check and found one of my girls missing. I stayed up eagerly waiting the return of my wayward student, and I checked with the night watchman many times after the 11:00 curfew to see if she had returned. Just in case of mistaken identify, I had taken my student's information sheet that contained her picture to show to the watchman. He maintained that she had not yet arrived. I asked him to tell my student to come to my room when she arrived, and he assured me that he would do that. In addition to knowing that she was safe, I also needed to know what condition she was in. Shortly after 2:00 A.M. I went to the lobby again to talk to the night watchman. At this time, he assured me that my student had arrived and that he had given her my message, but that she had decided to go to her room instead.

When I head this, I was incensed. "How dare she keep me awake worrying about her when she had decided to go to her room and sleep"! I ran to her room, pounded on the door, opened by her roommates, and found her fast asleep. I threw the covers off her and screamed at her for 5 minutes. Never in my life had I ever raised my voice like that. I called her parents in the U.S. and threatened to send her home immediately. I know that student tour companies can return disobedient students to the U.S. at their parents' expense. Had we been staying in Paris a little longer, I would have done so, but we were leaving Paris the next morning, and I certainly had to be with my group so I allowed her to stay.

However for the rest of the trip she was sullen and unresponsive. But she had plenty of time to conjure up a plausible explanation about why she did what she did. Her answer was that my group and I had gone off and left her. She didn't mention that she had conveniently got lost. That was at 10:30 P.M. That other group of "swingers" returned to the hotel at 1:00 A.M. She never did explain why she went to bed without checking in with me. By the time we returned home, she had convinced her parents that I was at fault. The problem with that was that she was one of my French IV students, and she still had to deal with me in class for the rest of the school year.

There was another small problem that I remember well. This time it was with one of my French IV boys, an excellent student. He wanted to take his friend along on our trip. His friend was not one of my students, but he was a student studying German at our school. Since he was best friends with my student, I allowed him to go with us. He also was under my umbrella of rules. One afternoon in Paris, the guide took us to the Fragonard Perfume Factory near the Opera. Fragonard also has another outlet in Grasse. The guides of Fragonard would take us through the building and show us how perfume and toilette water were made and packaged. Then at the end of the tour in the showroom, we were exposed to all kinds of fragrances. The neat thing about the Fragonard Factory was that they could imitate all the top selling perfumes. You simply told them that you wanted Chanel #5 for instance, and they offered you an aluminum bottle which read #5 with no mention of Chanel whatsoever. For obvious reasons the real name of the perfume was not revealed in print on the front of the bottle, but Fragonard had a very good imitation of the real thing. Yes, I know that this is not high on the list of every boy's list of things to do, but maybe he could get his mother, or his sister, or his girlfriend a unique souvenir.

My group was excited to go in, but my student's friend announced that they would not be going in. Instead they would be going out on their own. I felt sorry for my student, because now he is caught in the middle, going with his friend or going with his teacher. I knew the answer, of course, to his dilemma. I told my student's friend that if he chose to disobey me, that was his decision. But my student was staying with the group and me. End of discussion! I really felt that the friend needed my student's help since he spoke no French and had no training on the metro. Finally he acquiesced and joined the group, and his power play was disabled.

I had promised the parents before leaving that I would keep the students with me at all times, if possible. If they disobeyed me and I found out, I would report the problem to the parents when I got home. I, who was never married with any children of my own, was now a substitute parent for any student with me. The parents back home trusted me with their sons and daughters, knowing that I was a no-nonsense teacher and would continue this line of thought throughout the trip. Yes, of course, it was difficult to stay a step ahead of 8-10 students, and I am not sure that I succeeded one hundred percent.

You can only try to outthink them, but when they put their minds together, it is possible that they might win.

Every evening I checked them into their rooms according to the curfew that their parents requested—either 11 P.M. or midnight. Yes, they knew to stay in their rooms after the bed check. Does that mean that they did so? Who knows? Kids will be kids. However before I retired for the night, I made the rounds again, this time just listening at the door. I was hoping for silence, and that would mean that they went to sleep. If I heard talking with their roommate, that was not a problem.

What I didn't want to hear was a chorus of many voices all having a good time.

One night I found such a situation. One of the mini bar keys had slipped through my scrutiny, and there was a party going on after the bed check and without my invitation. One knock on the door brought complete silence. "Open up", I announced. Very reluctantly, they opened the door, and inside the room were most of my students. I announced that the party was over, and I would be around shortly to check them into their rooms again. I retrieved the bar key, locked the bar, and scooped up all the mini bottles of liquor that were out, and returned them to the hotel desk, but somehow they did not give the room credit for all the returns. Many were unopened and could be restocked. The next morning in the hotel lobby, the room with the open mini bar had a large liquor bill. I saw all the students dividing money to help pay, but no one ever announced that this was unfair. We were a little late leaving that morning, but I never got any complaints. After all, what part of drinking alcohol only in my presence, did they not understand? No one invited me to the party.

On another trip to France I had promised the students that on their last night in Paris I would take them to a popular stop on the Champs-Elysées called the "Drug Store". It bore an American name, and it had some of the same ideas. What we really wanted was their super sodas and sundaes. Everyone was looking forward to that. However fate has a way of interrupting even the best of plans. At that time we were staying in one of the many "quaint" French hotels. That means that there is a large staircase in the center of the hotel with a tiny elevator between the stairs. Also the rooms overlooked a rather large interesting roof and many of the students climbed around on the roof and used the roof as an entrance to their friends' rooms. I really was not aware that many of them were climbing around the rooftops until later.

On the last day one of my male students went to visit one of his new friends from another group, via the rooftop "entrance". When he stepped from the roof into the room, he needed to find a place to put his foot for stability. He chose the top of the toilet in his friend's bathroom. The toilet was old and broke from the foundation. Of course, the students weren't going to say anything about the broken toilet, but the maid reported it to the front desk which immediately notified the teachers. Now here is the problem. "Was my student totally responsible for the accident or was the student in the room equally responsible because he had invited him to enter via the rooftop"? The hotel didn't care who was responsible as long as someone paid for the toilet. So our last night in Paris was spent negotiating the price of a toilet instead of going to the "Drug Store". My student had money in his Emergency Fund, but the other student was really "broke".

After we finally negotiated the best price for a toilet, the other teacher involved loaned her student half of the money to be paid, and I deducted the other half from my student's Emergency Fund and paid for the balance. This whole procedure took the entire evening, and all the students who were not involved could not go out of the hotel unattended. All the students in both groups were really penalized since they spent the entire evening sitting in a boring hotel lobby waiting for the problem to be solved. "Good-bye, Drug Store". "Hello, Boredom". Traveling with students means that you have to have eyes in the back of your head. You never know what they are up to. You can barely close your eyes to sleep.

On another occasion I had a small group of advanced French students, all girls. They were eager to practice the French that they had been studying for the past four years. After we were settled in our hotel, I decided to take the girls to a church service since it was Easter, and there were many services in the churches. It needs to be stated here that the local boys knew where the student hotels were, and they also knew that many young Americans girls were staying in these hotels. So you could always count on a group of local boys hanging out at the entrance to the student hotels. They were eyeing the girls to see whom they might be able to attract. And of course our girls were eager to show off their knowledge of French. Getting the girls past the guys was a tricky situation. While waiting for all my girls to assemble, one of my senior girls was captivated by a tall Watusi dressed in full costume. He was tall and slender with a painted face and long colored feathers in his headdress. This was prior to the era where the Blacks and the Whites had intertwined their lives.

The Watusi announced that he and my student were going out. I immediately told him that was not going to happen. My student would be going to church with me. I can only imagine what her mother would have thought about her daughter going out on the town with her new "feathered" friend.

I did have other problems too numerous to mention, but I remember one unique problem. Every year in September I began looking for tours for the following spring. As best I could, I tried to diversify the listings by finding some place different within the French area. I found such a trip in 1991 with the student travel agency EF. It would be a trip to Paris, Versailles, Reims, Chantilly, Amboise, Chenonceaux, Angoulême, St. Emillion, Biarritz, and Saint-Jean-De-Luz, a beautiful seaside resort and active fishing port just across the French border in Spain. We would be spending 2 nights in nearby Biarritz.

Due to the Iraq War, I had lost several of my participants who had cancelled the trip because they were afraid to travel. This was not unique. Europe was starving for tourists who decided to stay home and travel at a future date. Consequently when we got to Biarritz most of the hotels were only partly filled, and we were housed in a first class complex called Domaine de Françon for two days. The complex included an anglo-normand style manor house like no other, with stained glass windows plus a golf course and tennis courts. We were only housed there because the hotels were hurting for travelers. This was certainly not a student hotel, and we were pleasantly surprised.

Our traveling group included 2 schools. I had 8 students and 2 adults with me. There was another group on our bus with 28 students. When we arrived in Biarritz, it was a balmy sunny day. The next day we were to travel to St. Jean de Luz, according to the itinerary, but the other group decided that on such a lovely day they wanted to go to the beach instead of following the itinerary. Our bus driver was Dutch, and he was very strict. He had certain guidelines and routines that he was not going to change. He said that he was not going to take my group to St. Jean de Luz when only 10 of us wanted to go. I was really upset. "How can part of a group sabotage the itinerary?" After much negotiation, the driver finally said he would drive us to the border, but he would not cross the border with the bus. Of all my many trips I never had a group of participants destroy the itinerary. Only a teenager would trade a day in the sun for a trip down the picturesque coast into Spain.

When we left Biarrtz, we continued the itinerary to Lourdes and the walled city of Carcassonne, then crossing the Pyranees to Barcelona, Spain. This was one of the most scenic trips ever offered to students I generally took small groups, usually just 8-10 students, and I was the only teacher. Most of them were my own students who had been with me for several years. They knew me, and I knew them. Also many of them were in my advanced French classes. Once in a while I took a French II student, but the advanced students benefited the most from the trips because they knew what to expect. As part of the curriculum, I would give my advanced students a Metro Test in class. Given a Metro map of Paris and a destination, they had to find the best way to get to the destination without taking the scenic route or getting lost. Even if they weren't going to Paris, they might be able to benefit from understanding the works of a subway system sometime in their lives.

Although the trips were designed for students, adults also could make the trip. The price was good. Sometimes it was a parent of one of the students, but more likely it was an adult who found out about the trip and decided to join us. However, it didn't matter how many adults were in the group, they were participants and not chaperones. I was the only chaperone on all trips. The parents and adults were to follow all of my guidelines with a few exceptions. Once in a while I accepted a French student from a nearby high school, but only on the recommendation of his French teacher. Taking my own students gave me an added edge, because once the trip was over, they still had to deal with me in class. A neighboring French student did not.

One important idea that I learned from the many student trips that I conducted to Europe was to keep the students off balance as much as possible. For example, my first student trip was a 10-day trip to Paris. Never again would I spend 10 days in the same city. That was way too long. The students knew the ropes after 2-3 days. After that trip, I chose trips that visited several cities. I spent no more than 2 days in Paris, then off to another city for 2 days, then off to another for 2 days. That way the students were kept off balance. They never felt comfortable in the new city. There was not enough time in the new city to know the ropes, or to know the "ins" and "outs" of the hotels. A ten-day stay in a foreign city allows the students to get ahead of you, and that's never a good idea.

Chapter Seventeen

1989 France's Bicentennial

In July, 1989, there was an opportunity to visit France and witness their 200-year celebration of the French Revolution. So I asked one of my friends if she would like to go with me. She said, "Yes", so we were off to Europe. Our trip started in England where some of the tall ships had begun to congregate. We stayed at the Tower Thistle Hotel, very near Tower Bridge so that we could see part of the parade of ships that would be participating in France's celebration. We had a week to visit some of the important tourist spots while in London, time to walk across Tower Bridge, walk around Piccadilly Circus, visit the pubs, and still have a ringside seat to the Cutty Sark Parade of Ships en route to France. There was also time to lunch at Covent Gardens, see the Clarence Bull Exhibit at the National Portrait Gallery, the Rosetta Stone, the Elgin Marbles, and the Lindow Man Skeleton at the British Museum, visit the Tate Art Gallery which contains a splendid exhibit of Picassos masterpieces, plus Rodin's *The Kiss*, and still have time to join the queue for tickets to *Les Misérables*. For tickets, we had to spend one afternoon sitting on the curb. This was not a new experience for me. On a prior visit to London, I had spent the entire day sitting on the curb for tickets to *Phantom of the Opéra*.

One afternoon there was even time to take a boat ride on the Thames to visit Greenwich with time to walk around the village and see where the Greenwich Meridian begins. There was also time to visit the Tower of London and see the Beefeaters and their collection of Ravens.

At the end of the week we were off to France. We departed from London City Airport on a De Haviland Dash 7. I had visited Heathrow and Gatwick Airports before, and I really didn't know about a third airport. It was a well-kept secret. However I fell in love with this small well-hidden airport. It had a Duty Free Shop plus other small shops. Plus there was no crowd whatsoever, just a small group of passengers flying to Paris. The plane served us a delicious lunch complete with wine and an after-lunch Grand Marnier. An added plus was that the plane was flying at a low altitude so that we could see England and France from the air. We landed at Roissy Airport near Paris and checked into the Méridien Montparnasse Hotel.

France was all-ablaze in celebration. The streets were all decorated in Blue, White, and Red with costumes, parades, and flyovers. The TV in our room featured the Revolution Festivities. I went out on the evening of the 13th to view all the various celebrations. My roommate was too frightened to accompany me so she stayed in the room. At times the French can be a little carried away with themselves, but I had witnessed many French celebrations before, and I was not going to stay in our room and watch the celebrations on TV.

While in Paris, we visited the Montparnasse Cemetery where François Rude, Guy de Maupassant, and Frédéric Bartholdi are buried, along with other important notables. We also visited Picpus Cemetery where Lafayette's tomb is

189

located. I showed my roommate the tomb of Ste. Catherine Labouré on Rue du Bac. The weather was beautiful. It was such a joy to walk along the Seine. We also took a Bateau Mouche ride. All of this before traveling to Rouen to view the finale of *Les Voiles de la Liberté!* Translation: the Sails of Liberty, a grand flotilla of all the schooners and tall ships from all over the world. This was an exceptional maritime experience exhibiting 23 magnificent sailing ships from Poland, the U.S.S.R., Argentina, Italy, Norway, Mexico, Venezuela, the U.S., Uruguay, Bulgaria, England, and Sweden. All of these countries had sent their tall ships to France to help in celebrating France's Bicentennial. The U.S. sent *the Eagle* and *the Endeavor* to participate in this grandiose experience. The Parade Of Tall Ships was fabulous, a unique get together of tall ships from around the world. What a way to celebrate France's Bicentennial! My head was dizzy from viewing all the beautiful tall ships.

Before returning to the U.S. we visited Monet's home and gardens at Giverny. On our last day we caught the TGV to Dijon, a city famous for its mustard. Before we checked out, our Paris hotel gave us a large poster of the Rights of Man and Citizens as a souvenir of our fantastic visit to Paris during their bicentennial celebration. It hangs on my wall today, a framed souvenir of my favorite country.

Chapter Eighteen

1993 Musicals & Ireland

My second summer after retirement I wanted to do something different In Europe. London is so well known for its theater district. I had always tried to see a musical whenever I was in London, but seldom had time. However in the spring of 1993 I took a trip to London just to see the musicals. Then I would attach it to an organizd trip of Ireland afterwards. I left April 16, for a flight to Chicago, then on to London, Heathrow. When I landed I took an Airbus into the city, and the driver let me out at the shortest distance to the Winchester Hotel where I thought I would be staying for the next five days. However the hotel was fully booked so they sent me to the Pavillion Hotel instead. My room was like a postage stamp, but I was there to see the musicals, not to stay in a room, so I headed out for the theatre district.

My first musical was *Starlight Express*, and my ticket only cost £5 or about $8.00. I would always ask for the Senior Citizen Rate, a process that London seems to have. Then I got tickets for *Buddy* also at the special price of £12 or $19.50. Next I got tickets for *Joseph & the Amazing Technicolor Dreamcoat* for £15 or about $24.00. Then I got tickets to the *City of Angels* for £12.50, about $21.00. Next I got senior citizen tickets for *Blood Brothers* for £11.50, about $18.00, followed by tickets *to Kiss of the Spider Woman* at £10, or about $16.00. Then I joined the queue for *Phantom of the Opera.* I was second in line and after 3 hours in line I got a ticket for £28, about $45. Three hours in line was much better than the last time I saw it when I sat on the curb for most of the day to see this musical. This time the theatre stopped making the tourists spend the day outside waiting until curtain time. Whenever any tickets were returned, they now sold them to those in the queue right away. This was a more humane procedure. My final musical was *Robinhood, Prince of Sherwood.* For this musical I got a £20 ticket reduced to £10, about $16.00. Eight musicals in five days kept me very busy in London.

After my musical excursion, I got a cab to Heathrow and flew Air Lingus to Dublin. Before leaving the U.S., I had made plans to join a Globus Tour of Ireland when my theater days were finished. However just 10 minutes before we landed in Dublin, the luggage handlers went out on strike. We had to wait a considerable time to retrieve out luggage. In Dublin I met the other tourists who were traveling with me. Our Globus Tour of Ireland was by bus. We stopped at Trinity College to see the Book of Kells, a beautiful old manuscript illustrating the four gospels in calligraphy dating from around the 9th century. The next morning we visited the Irish National Stud Farm at Kildare then to the Rock of Cashel where St. Patrick preached after he banished Satin from a nearby cave. Afterwards we drove to Tipperary and Limerick and Shannon. Our second night was spent in Ennis.

The next morning it was not surprising that we had tea and scones for breakfast. Now we would visit Galway Bay, and nearby we would visit a lamb farm. The next morning found us touring the countryside, ending up at Bunratty

Castle where we had a delicious Irish dinner, followed by a lot of singing, white wine, and mead. Next, we drove along lots of bogs where we got a ferry at Killimer to cross the Shannon River, and continued to Tralee, then a 100 mile drive around the Ring of Kerry.

The next day we were off to Killarney for a group photo. Then we went to the medieval Blarney Castle where we could opt to kiss the Blarney Stone if we chose to do so. That according to the legend would give us the "Gift of Gab". From Blarney we drove to Cork, a city a little like Amsterdam, but the canals were now covered over. From Cork we drove to Waterford via Youghal, a beautiful costal resort where *Moby Dick* was filmed. Sir Walter Raleigh lived here before he died in the Tower of London. That evening was spent with an $18.00 optional trip to Passge East, a small fishing village on the bank of Waterford Harbour. We spent the first part of the evening in a local pub with an Irish guitarist and a couple of glasses of wine before returning to the Tower Hotel for an 8:00 P.M. dinner.

The next day we stopped at Glendalough Monastery then on to a visit of Powerscourt House and Gardens. We spent an hour visiting the beautiful gardens there. Later we checked in to the Montrose Hotel, and since this was our last evening in Ireland, we treated ourselves to a $60.00 dinner at a nearby cabaret. The next morning early we caught a cab for the airport and a return visit home. Our flight took us back to Heathrow, then on to Chicago via British Air. I had requested a window seat but did not get it because there was a large group traveling together who wanted to sit together. To replace the window seat, the stewardess took me to an upper cabin and gave me an aisle seat. The upper cabin had only 24 seats and was really plush, with individual TV's and a choice of several movies. All economy class receives knit slippers, a toothbrush, toothpaste, and eyeshades. The movie was *"A Few Good Men"*. I also saw *"Hoffa"*. This was a pleasant end to a pleasant trip.

Chapter Nineteen

1993-2008 Bicycle Trips in Europe

Most of my trips abroad were made while I was still teaching since I had the entire summer to travel. However when I retired, I searched for other hobbies. I took up singing, knitting, bowling, and biking. Biking could be combined with traveling so I searched for a combination of both. I found it with Elderhostel. So in the summer of 1993, I began my first of thirteen bicycle trips in Europe. The first eleven included North Holland, the Loire Valley, the Danube, Denmark, East Anglia, Bordeaux (the Basque Coast), the Salzach and Inn Rivers, South Holland, Italy and Austria, the Cotswolds and Chalk Downs, and Provence.

Biking in Europe is a treat. Many of the European countries have really lovely bike paths where you can enjoy the countryside without the noise of the traffic. I didn't find that the case in Italy however. Once when biking along an Italian highway, the traffic was so intense that when the trucks passed me, my helmet rose several inches off my head. But that was a unique situation. The biking experience is great, but you would not want to take a bike trip if you have not seen the target country first because what you see of the country are the back roads and small villages. The big cities are ignored.

The plus side of biking through Europe is that it allows you to meet with the villagers as you bike through their area.

In Holland it is so peaceful biking through the countryside along the canals through the land of windmills and tulips. The terrain is flat and makes biking easy except when biking along the North Sea when the wind coming off the North Sea is a factor to be reckoned with. The wind is usually a factor in biking. When you are biking against the wind, it's as though you are biking up hill. When the wind is at your back, you barely need to peddle. Then if you are in a cross wind, you may have to lean into the wind to avoid being blown over.

I recommend biking in the months of May or September because the tourists are there in June, July, and August. September is safer than May because it is warmer. On some of my May bike trips I found myself biking in a lot of rain and even some sleet. That made it difficult for me since I have Raynaud's Disease where the blood supply to the hands and feet is temporarily blocked by exposure to the cold. When that happens, I must find a place right away to warm my hands and feet since circulation stops in the extremities. Biking with no feeling in your hands or feet can be dangerous. On two occasions I found myself in that situation, and I had to ask the guide to find a rest stop so that I could get feeling back in my hands and feet. At one stop in England the guide found me an inside swimming pool where I could dangle my feet to get them warm.

On my trip to Italy and Austria in 2000, a very amusing event happened to me. In the morning we had biked to Cremona, a very interesting Italian town famous for its Stradivarius instruments. We visited the museum where they have many of the tools used by Antonio Stradivari, and we had a lecture on violin making and an explanation about the violin collection owned by the City of Cremona. We also had a visit to one of the numerous violin shops. The city of Cremona has a collection of violins housed in its city hall plus they have a giant bell tower attached to the Cremona Cathedral. The tower ranks third in height for brickwork bell towers in the world. Since we were in Cremona for lunch, I thought it would be a good idea to climb to the top of the tower to get a good view of the city. So I bought a ticket at the entrance from a man who was not only selling tickets but also was selling souvenirs and postcards.

The view of the city from the top of the tower was wonderful. I took several pictures before deciding to go down. When I got to the bottom of the steps the iron gate leading to the tower was closed and locked, and the little man who sold me my ticket was nowhere in sight. All his souvenirs were covered with a large white cloth. There was another couple locked in the tower with me. I did not know them, but we soon became friends. We shouted for help, but to no avail. The townspeople stopped by to look at us. I'm sure that they considered us just another trio of dumb illiterate tourists. Eventually we shouted to the group watching, "Please call the police!" Eventually the police showed up, and sized up the situation. Then they left to go get the ticket taker who was home having lunch. He arrived much later with a key to unlock the gate all the while mumbling to himself and pointing to a sign that announced that the tower would be closing from noon until 2:00 P.M. Anyone who was paying attention could have seen the hours of closing. But a tourist is not always reading the fine print. We entered the tower at 11:50. A.M. It would have been helpful if the ticket taker had advised us that we only had 10 minutes to see everything.

Photo #45

Photo #46

Photo #45 shows me locked in the tower. Photo #46 shows the 2 police officers who rescued us plus the ticket taker holding the sign with the visitation hours of the tower. The other woman is the one also locked in with me in the tower, and the woman's husband took our picture as a reminder of what happens when you're not paying close attention when you travel. My biking group would have been inconvenienced had I been unable to escape on time.

After my bicycle trip to Provence, France, during the summer of 2002, I made a stark realization. These bike trips were getting harder and harder for me. Provence does not seem so hilly while sitting in a bus or in a car, but on the seat of a bicycle it seemed almost impossible. Provence was my 11th bicycle trip, and that was 10 years after retirement. I loved the bicycle trips. The pluses were that they furnished the bikes, the hotels, and the sightseeing, the breakfasts and evening meals. The minuses were that given an itinerary and dates you had to bike from Point A to Point B on a certain day. It didn't matter if it were raining that day. Also the wind didn't matter. Your health may have mattered a little, but you were to be on your bicycle for the entire trip. Usually the daily distances were 25 to 40 miles, but you had most of the day to do this.

After Provence, I found out that Elderhostel had a much easier group of bicycle trips. There were bicycle/barge trips. Now you had daily options of whether you wanted to do the daily bike ride or whether you wanted to stay on the barge. Staying on the barge was not very interesting, I must admit. There was little to do while traveling through the locks. But if a certain day were extremely difficult or if the weather were cold and rainy, you now had another option. So you might ask the guide to let you know when the most difficult biking day was, and you could opt to stay on board.

So my last 2 bicycle trips were bicycle/barge trips to the Rhine and Mosel Rivers of Germany, and Paris and the châteaux of Central France. But as I got older, even they got harder so on my last trip when I felt weak and faint, I was persuaded by my friend to stop biking in Europe. Yes, you did have a guide with you, and you did have a group of about 20 bikers to ride with you, but basically you were on your own. And as one gets older, that seems a little scary. If you got sick or fell, you might have to stay in Europe all by yourself until you got well enough to get home.

Chapter Twenty

Problems With Biking Roommates

I really only had one problem with a roommate when I started the bicycle trips. I once had a roommate who snored all night long. The bike trips are hard enough, and you really need a good night's sleep to do your best. I could not sleep with all the noise that she was putting out. I tried putting my bedding in the tub in the bathroom. That didn't work. As a last resort, I took my bedding and slept in the hallway outside my room. Sometimes I could even hear the noise through the door, and I would have to move my bedding down the hall. Sleeping in the hallway is not a good idea. Plus it's not safe. I told the guide about my problem, and sometimes he was able to get me a separate room in our hotel, if a room were available. But had this happened on a barge, there was no extra room. The bicycle/barge trips were always limited to the number of bedrooms on the barge, usually 10. That meant that the maximum number of cyclists was 20, two per room. No singles were available. For my 13 bicycle trips, I almost always had a roommate. Sometimes that was a good experience; sometimes, not.

International Bicycle Trips which runs the Elderhostel bicycle trips has very strict rules. You must be able to guide your bike in motion and at the same time look backwards over your left shoulder. You must complete a test ride when in Europe and in front of the guide showing that you can safely mount and dismount your bike. You are given a list of road signs that you will encounter along the way, and you are expected to memorize them and follow them. Also everyday at the beginning of the morning ride, the guide chooses a person who will be "Sweep" for the day. A "Sweep'" will always be the last person in the line of bikers, and it is his job to see that no one gets lost. Also the sweep should be a fairly strong biker. You would not want the weakest biker to be the last one in line. On all my bicycle trips there was only one occasion that a couple of bikers got lost. The idea is that the "sweep" acts as a broom to sweep up any misguided bikers. It is thought to be a compliment to be chosen "sweep". I was chosen sweep several times on my bicycle trips. (Photo #47)

Photo #47

My 13th bicycle trip had an unusual problem. I had the roommate from hell. She was a non-stop talker, telling me all about her various husbands and friends, things that I really didn't care about. Also she was a marginal biker. On one occasion she failed to notice a major road sign that announced that we should yield to merging traffic. We were just reaching the top of a hill when she made a right turn in front of a car which had the right of way. The bikers went around her, and she continued biking with just a minimal stop to regain her balance. She had scraped the car slightly, but I guess she felt that it was not a problem. And it wasn't, until the end of the day at the barge. There waiting for her was the couple with the damaged car. Two things were wrong. In France whenever there is an accident, both parties must stop and wait for the police to fill out an accident form. That didn't happen since my roommate barely stopped. Also there was a matter of insurance. The couple wanted the name of my roommate's insurance company so that they could file a claim.

Then later in the trip my roommate failed to negotiate a roundabout. I must admit the roundabouts are everywhere in Europe, and they are tricky, but we were given special instructions on how to enter and exit a roundabout. On every bicycle trip, a great deal of attention is always paid to reading road signs and rules of the road. Well, she got caught in the center of one of the roundabouts and could not get off due to the traffic surrounding her. As a last resort she began screaming until the group stopped and helped her exit. That was the last straw for the guide, and he removed her from the biking group and put her in the driver's van along with all of our luggage for the remainder of the tour. That meant that she missed the beautiful forest and castle of Rambouillet because the car and driver always took the most direct route, not the scenic bicycle route.

These two items did not affect me directly; however some things did. For example, she always got up early in the morning and went to our bathroom to clean out her nasal passages. That involved a lot of gargling, gurgling, and snorting for 10 minutes, an irritation to my ears. The bathrooms on the barges are not soundproof.

Also, the bikers liked to take a walk through the small villages after dinner, but we always had to wait for her to put on her makeup, eye shadow, rouge, and lipstick along with her pashmina wrap before we started out. We went to see the village. I don't know whom she thought she was going to meet. We were in biker's gear out to see the sights, not to impress the natives. Those were just small irritants along with her constant babbling.

On one evening stroll we discovered that we both were spending an extra 3 days in Paris at the end of the bike trip. I had already booked a hotel room for my three days; she had not. So we decided to spend it together in the same hotel room to cut down on our expenses. Our first morning in Paris, following the bike trip, she asked me to make her a cup of tea with my emersion spoon. She had watched me make my hazelnut coffee every day during the bicycle trip. I had never offered to make her any drink, but being a good roommate, I fixed her a cup of tea; she got dressed early and went downstairs to the lobby. She had seen a computer in the lobby, and she wanted to send some emails to friends back home. So off she went with her cup of tea.

Twenty minutes later, I heard a knock at the door. She appeared and announced that she had lost everything. At first I didn't know what she was saying, but I soon found out. It seems that she had taken her cup of tea and her large purse downstairs with her and had put her purse beside her in a chair. She was so intent while working on the Internet that she failed to notice a man who also was in the lobby. He noticed her inattention and kept moving closer and closer to her, chair by chair. At last he laid his coat over her purse, and when she failed to notice that, he picked up his coat and her purse and left the hotel. So now she was penniless with no passport, credit cards, money, plane tickets or souvenirs. It was the weekend, and all banks were closed in the U.S.

She now became my responsibility. She had no money for anything so I became her banker. I paid for the meals, transportation, museum fees, lunches, dinners, passport replacement fee, and the hotel bill that we were going to split. Yes, I kept records, and when we both got back to the U.S., I did get reimbursed. But the trauma was awful. The wear and tear on my nerves could not be reimbursed. We know how the theft happened because the hotel had a video showing how it was accomplished. But part of my time was spent escorting her to the police station to fill out a report. I could speak French, and she needed my help to explain to the officers what had happened. I had things that I wanted to see in Paris, and the police station was not one of them. I did loan her the $60.00 she needed for a new passport. But I did not accompany her to the Embassy. I got her a metro map, and indicated how to get there and where to get off. But I was not going to spend my last 3 days making up for her stupidity. Why did she take her purse downstairs in the first place? Had she left it in the room, we could have avoided all of these disruptions. But I knew how bad she felt because I had undergone a similar experience in Amsterdam. I must admit that I was extremely glad to get home after that. So as we were walking around Paris, we stumbled upon this statue that seemed to be in similar difficulty. I couldn't pass by without having my picture taken side-by-side with a statue that also seems to be down in the dumps. (Photo #48)

Photo #48

Chapter Twenty-one

Pickpockets

In September, 1999, on my 8th bicycle trip, I had made arrangement to arrive a day early in Amsterdam in order to meet some friends that I had previously met on the Austrian Bike Trip. The four of us decided that we would enroll together on the South Holland trip the following year.

I arranged to get to Amsterdam the day before the start of the bike trip to meet with my 3 friends. When I got to the hotel, I found a note from them asking me to meet them at the Rijksmuseum as soon as possible. So I put down all my bags and headed out for the museum. I soon found them near Rembrandt's Night *Watch*. After the museum visit, they said they wanted to go to the Flower Fair. That sounded good so I joined them. Then they announced that they were taking Tram #5 so I joined them. Now I must admit, I never take streetcars or trams, if at all possible. Actually the Flower Fair was only a few blocks away and quite walkable, but I was not in charge of this expedition. My gal friend and I sat down and the two men stood up at the other end of the tram. Yes, it was crowded, but we didn't have far to go. As soon as we got off, one of the men asked if we had seen the pickpockets on the tram. As soon as I heard that I reached back for my fanny pack, and it was unzipped and all my valuables were gone. The friend who had seen the pickpockets had actually felt the pickpocket's hand in his pocket, and was able to tell him to remove his hand. Why didn't he announce "Pickpockets aboard!"? After all, he was part of the three I was meeting in Amsterdam.

So now I had lost my passport, my Dutch money, my American money, my credit cards, my plane tickets, even my Traveler's Checks. In addition to losing my composure, I was devastated. My bicycle trip had not yet started and I had lost everything. I knew better than to take crowded trams or any trams at all. I had given lectures to my students on how to avoid thieves and scams. However I was so engaged in the conversation with my friend that I dropped my guard. So the rest of the day and evening I spent in the police station recounting the theft. I was so stressed out, but even in the midst of chaos, I conjured up the exact number of my main credit card that was stolen. Of course I cancelled all cards, but I did not have the list of T.C. numbers with me. The list was at home on the desk. But I was not worried about the T.C's. I could always get reimbursed later at home. Also I was not worried about meals. Breakfast and dinner for the next two weeks was included in the trip. Also I had a box of granola bars that I had brought along for lunch, and those along with my water bottle would see me through the day. So I filled out a police report, and they advised me to call them every day during the trip to see if anyone had turned in my passport case.

I found it very interesting that another victim on the tram also suffered a similar loss. A local man had his carry-on hanging in front of him while he was reading a newspaper. He was reading his morning news while standing in the aisle. He was a native who rode this tram everyday, and he also lost all his money. So this just proves that the thieves are really very good at their trade.

I called my friend back home and told him what had happened. During the next few days it was hard to hold back the tears. I had never been victimized before so this was a totally new experience. When asked if I wanted someone to send me money, I replied "No". If I were stupid enough to get blitzed by the thieves, then I deserved to suffer a little or a lot as the case may be. I called around to a few agencies, but no one offered to lend me any money. Even the embassy will make you a new passport, but at a $60.00 charge. That was the only time I borrowed money, just to get a passport. The airlines also were not very cooperative. I went to the airport to try to get some assurance that they would fly me back to the states at the end of my bike trip. They assured me that my tickets could not be used by the thieves, but they would not assure me that I could fly home without them.

So when the bicycle trip began, I joined the group. However, every day when we stopped for lunch, usually in a small village, I went to the local police station and asked them to call the Amsterdam Police to see if my passport case had been found. The answer was always, "No"

However the natives in Amsterdam and Holland were very sympathetic about my situation. They did not like the idea that a visitor in their country could be scammed. One might say that they were almost embarrassed. They are so proud of their country, and a thing like this gives them a black eye. At the hotel in Amsterdam, I would go down to the lobby late at night to see if anything of mine had surfaced. I was usually very emotional, and the night clerk would always put me through to my friend in the U.S. free of the telephone charge.

Also on one occasion we bikers were promised a special visit to a pastry shop. During the bicycle trip, we usually had some special stop, generally an ice cream store. When we stopped at the pastry shop, the owner served everyone. But when he got to me, I told him that I was sorry, but I could not buy anything from him. He also took pity on me and gave me a large pastry free of charge. I wasn't looking for handouts, but when asked I would relate the happenings in Amsterdam.

Midway through the trip, Elderhostel sent a car and driver to my hotel. They were not going to leave me stranded abroad. The driver took me to the Embassy in Amsterdam and along with the $60.00, that I had borrowed from my biker friend, I got a replacement passport. The driver waited for me and returned me to the group in the afternoon. The only thing I missed was a day of biking.

We think the theft was done by a group of gypsies. The men would take the wallet, then take what they wanted, and pass it off to their wives or girlfriends for the remainder of the stolen goods. Finally at the end of the trip in Amsterdam, I went to the airport. As long as I had a police report, Delta was willing to fly me back home since I had a copy of my ticket. So now I had everything that I needed, my passport and my plane tickets.

Now for the rest of the story. I got home safely, and my friend picked me up as usual at the Cincinnati Airport. As soon as I arrived home, I listened to my phone messages.

Near the end of all my messages, a foreign girl with broken English announced, "I have your passport. What to do with it"

I was not very enchanted with this news. My credit cards had been cancelled. I was home so I didn't need my passport or plane tickets, but there were some things that I would like to have returned: my passport case, my driver's license, my credit cards, my social security card, and my travelers checks. So just when I was thinking about closing this chapter of my life, it was open again.

The caller left her phone number in Amsterdam on the answering machine, so I called her. She told me that she had found my passport case in a garbage can, and she would return it to me if I sent her $30.00 reimbursement for the postage. So I told her that I would send her a check in that amount after I received the stolen passport case. Then she said that that wouldn't work since she was not legal in Holland; therefore she had no checking account or references.

Now I'm smart enough to know that dropping a $20.00 bill along with a $10.00 bill in an envelope is not a good idea. I never send cash through the mail. But what other solution did I have? So when I received my passport case from her, I did what she wanted. I put the $30.00 cash in an envelope and sent it to the address that she had given me. My returned passport case contained my passport, my plane tickets, my credit cards, and my driver's license, and my health cards—all of which had either been cancelled or replaced. But, I did find it interesting, however, that the American Express Traveler's Checks were not returned in my passport case. They kept them, for whatever purpose, I don't know.

211

A week later at 2:00 A.M., I got another call from her. The operator wanted to know if I would accept the charges from Amsterdam. I thought about it for a minute. Then I decided that the thief's girlfriend had nothing that I wanted to hear. I was sorry if she didn't get the money. I suspected that it would be stolen. I told the operator "No". The first phone call had already cost me $35.00, and I had no intention of spending any more money on my lost things.

After 20 minutes, at 2:20 A.M., I got another call from the international operator asking me again if I would accept the charges. Once again I told her "No". I think this was a perfect example of the boyfriend taking what he wanted from my passport case, then passing it off to his girl friend, and she could "milk" it for what she could. Well, that was the end of that fiasco. At home, I located the numbers of my traveler's checks, and American Express reimbursed me for the full amount. Also because I had the police report along with many receipts, my insurance company covered the rest of my expenses, even the phone charges from Amsterdam and the $60.00 passport fee. But the wear and tear on my nerves was not something that I could recover.

A note to future travelers: the scams and thefts in Europe are rampant. The thieves try to fall down in front of you, often with their children, and when you trip over them or try to avoid tripping over them, that's when they relieve you of your possessions.

Another trick that they use is done with an imitation gold ring. A pair of thieves works this scam together, usually a man and a woman. The man spots you as a tourist, and he walks along beside you but just out of your range of vision.

He then tosses the ring to a spot in front of you when his accomplice appears, picks up the worthless ring, and asks if it belongs to you. Since it doesn't, she suggests that since the owner can't be found, the next best thing is to split the "find" between the two of you. Since the ring can't be divided, she suggests that you keep the ring, but give her half of the money that the ring is worth, usually about $25.00+. A twosome tried this routine on me in the Tuileries Garden in Paris. The usual tourist feels really rushed. He is busy looking at monuments and trying to squeeze as much in as possible in the allotted time. However if given the time, it is very interesting to watch the various schemes take place. Just find yourself a bench in the Tuileries and just "people watch". A good rule of thumb is not to stop walking when accosted by a stranger. Look straight ahead, keep walking, and ignore them keeping your hand on your wallet.

Chapter Twenty-two

Traveling With My Friend

I have not recounted every one of my 45 trips abroad. I grouped the student tours and only related the experiences that were different. I have marked 45 trips because I have a few diaries with daily notes about cities that I visited and dates, but no year, so I cannot place them in any sequence. With so many trips in my brain, they will have to remain a mystery. For this final chapter, I got the chance to travel with my lifelong friend. For the first 43 trips, he had taken me to the airport and picked me up, taken care of Muffet, my Bichon Frisé, and Missey, my Moluccan Cockatoo. That enabled me to travel without worrying about my pets. However, after the death of my pets, I really wanted to show him my favorite country, France.

It's hard to explain why I love France so much. Perhaps it's because I can speak the language. Perhaps it's because it is so filled with fascinating history and monuments. The bottom line is that I never tire of visiting France. Seeing the monuments again is like reuniting with old friends. Most of the 45 trips included a visit to Paris at the beginning, at the end, or in the middle.

When I asked my friend if he would accompany me on a future trip to France, he said that he would if I could find a two-week tour of just France. I told him that I thought I could do that, and I did. So in the fall of 2010, the two of us took a

Grand European Tour of just France. We added a couple of extra days in Paris to see the sites that I thought he would enjoy.

So we visited Nôtre Dame, the Louvre, Cluny Museum, the Marmottan Museum, Napoleon's Tomb, and the Sacré Coeur. An evening boat ride on the Seine was included in our tour. Our tour also included a trip to the Palace of Versailles. We were lucky because it was Sunday and the fountains were all working.

I like the way that Paris divides its train stations. They are basically grouped by direction. The trains going southwest and west leave from Gare Montparnasse. Those going east depart from Gare de l'Est. Those going north depart from Gare du Nord. Trains departing for the southeast of France leave from Gare de Lyon. This is an over-simplification of their system, but it is interesting to note that it seems to be a very organized way of train travel.

Our trip began with a train ride on the TGV (the Train de Grande Vitesse) from Gare de Lyon. We left the train when it arrived in Avignon, which is famous for the Palais des Papes where the popes lived during their reign in France. The city is also known for the children's song, *Sur le Pont d'Avignon* where they dance. You can still dance on the bridge, but that's about all you can do. Today the Pont d'Avignon or as it is called le Pont St.-Benézet is the bridge to nowhere since it ends in the middle of the Rhone River. In this same area is the famous Pont du Gard, the old aqueduct, built by the Romans in the first century, which brought water down from the mountains to the city of Nîmes. It is so massive and beautiful that it makes you realize that the Romans were not only great builders but also excellent architects.

Photo #49

From Avignon, we got our motor coach, which took us to Nice where we stayed for 2 nights. After dinner we took an optional trip to Monte Carlo where for 10 euros each we could visit the famous casino. What a disappointment! I had seen the casino many years before at the height of its glory. Now it was just a shadow of what it once was. There was little activity transpiring there this time—only one Blackjack table operating and only 2 tourists playing Blackjack. There were a few other gamblers, but quite a few were just standing around doing nothing. The interior of the building is still beautiful and quite interesting to see, but there is little going on there today except perhaps for the girls sitting on the benches inside looking for clients.

The next day on our route to the hilltop town of St. Paul de Vence, we stopped at the Fragonard Factory at Grasse where I bought a small bottle of Mimosa cologne. Then we continued to St. Paul de Vence. There is a private art museum there, but instead we visited the small cemetery where the artist Marc Chagall is buried. Dinner that night was in a small family restaurant called Chez Cotton.

The next morning our private bus took us to Nîmes, famous for its Roman amphitheatre. We had a rest stop here so we opted to see the Arènes for 7.80 euros each. While we were in Nîmes, I tried to find the gardens with the Chained Floral Crocodile. The crocodile was a pattern on the hillside attached to a beautiful chain of flowers. I had seen it many years before when I showed it to my students. But now it was nowhere to be found. The garden was still there, but no *Crocodile Enchaîné* as it used to be called.

After a photo stop at la Maison Carrée, we were off to the walled city of Carcassonne where we had a tour of the city. This city looks as though it just emerged from a fairy tale with all its walls and turrets. I was glad to be back in this ancient city where I had first stayed at the Hôtel de la Cité. I loved this hotel not only because it bordered the ancient walls, but also because it contained many hanging tapestries by Fabrice, a local artist who lived in a nearby village. When I saw the Hotel again, I had to enter and inquired about the beautiful Fabrice tapestries.

Fabrice's tapestries used to be everywhere in the hotel. They were beautiful and so vivid in color. The subject matter was usually a floral design. After my first visit to Carcassonne, I had written the artist, Fabrice, and asked him if he could design a tapestry for me, one that had French Poodles as its theme. That was the only requirement. For the rest of the design, I gave him *carte blanche* to do whatever he wanted. Fabrice designed that tapestry for me and sent it by air. It now hangs in my living area, and it became the centerpiece of all my furniture.

Now when I returned to the hotel where I had first seen his work, I eagerly inquired at the desk about the Fabrice Tapestries that used to be hanging everywhere on their walls. The walls were now bare, and they hadn't a clue what I was talking about. No one had ever seen the many beautiful wall hangings by Fabrice. Even today, the only memory I can find about the artist Fabrice is hanging on my great room wall.

Our hotel for the two night's stay was Hôtel Des Trois Couronnes. It was outside the walls, but at night the walls and towers of Carcassonne were illuminated, and the city resembled a beautiful fairyland. We toured the city of Carcassonne, and the following morning we had an all-day tour of the nearby city of Albi with its unique cathedral dedicated to Sainte Cécile.

From Carcassonne we traveled to Lourdes, site of the visions of Sainte Bernadette. The Miraculous Grotto no longer held the dozens of crutches that the lame used to leave after their cure. Perhaps there were too many crutches to continue this process, or maybe it became just too much clutter for the miracle Grotto. We were not there long enough to witness the evening candlelight procession around this miraculous site, but we were there long enough to see the sick and the lame who had come to the city seeking a cure.

From Lourdes we traveled through Bordeaux, then on to the Courvoisier Cognac Distillery at Jarnac, where we were treated to a tour and a sample of their famous cognac. Then we were off to Blois for dinner.

Our destination was now the château country. Our first stop was the château of Chambord, then Amboise, then Chenonceau. At Chambord we only had a photo stop since a tour of the chateau would take all day. At Amboise we toured the château, then saw the small chapel where Leonard de Vinci is entombed. At Chenonceau we toured not only the château but also the beautiful gardens. Our evening meal was at the *Château* de Beaulieu.

The next morning we left for Mont. St. Michel, that beautiful Benedictine Abbey which stands on an islet just off the Normandy Coast.

According to the legend, Michel, the archangel appeared to St. Aubert and asked him to build a church on this spot. Visiters to the Mont are warned about the scheduled arrival of the tides which surround the Mont.

Next on our list of tourist spots was Bayeux to see the famous Bayeux Tapestry which depicts the Norman conquest of England in 1066. Tickets for viewing the tapestry were 5.20 euros each. I had heard and read about this tapestry many times, but I was surprised at its length. The intricate detail of the tapestry is outstanding.

Our next visit was to Arromanches, Omaha Beach, and the American Cemetery where more than 9,000 American soldiers are buried. It is a very solemn experience, walking among all these white crosses, some with names, some, without. Unlike Père la Chaise, where there are many grand tombstones of famous people who left their footprints in history, this cemetery had many identical simple markers of many many young men who had given up their lives to defeat evil. This they did so that we could have freedom. We stayed for the evening closing ceremony when they take down the American flag and play taps. It was very impressive—the utter quietness along with the lowering of our flag. Also nearby is the little town of Sainte-Mère-Eglise where one of the American paratroopers landed on the roof of the church during the June, 1944, Normandy Invasion. A replica of the jumpers parachute hangs on the roof of the church today as a reminder.

The next morning we were off to Rouen where there is another beautiful Gothic cathedral. There is also an astronomical clock at the entrance to the old city. I wanted to revisit the square where Jeanne d'Arc was burned at the stake. After Jeanne had helped win the battles making it possible for Charles VII to be crowned king of France, she was captured by the Burgundians and sold to the English, who accused her of heresy and forever sealed her fate. Charles did nothing to try to save her. So goes royal gratitude! When I was here in the 60's, there was a beautiful square commemorating this historical event. Today on the Place du Vieux Marché stands a very beautiful modern church dedicated to Ste. Jeanne. However it was lunchtime when we arrived, and the church was closed for the 2-3 hour optional lunchtime closing.

Before arriving in Paris, we had one more important stop to make—Giverny, the home and gardens of Claude Monet. We had 2 hours to spend strolling through the gardens and visiting his home. Inside his house, the dishes reflect the beautiful blue/yellow combination.

This was our last day of the trip so when we arrived back in Paris, we were treated to our farewell dinner at *Les Noces de Jeannette* Restaurant. We had three choices for each course, and there were many courses.

My friend and I had added a few days in Paris after the tour so that we could see some of the sites that we had missed. Our first stop was the Hôtel Biron, Rodin's home and gardens, now called Musée Rodin. I was particularly interested in seeing and photographing *le Penseur, Les Bourgeois de Calais, la Porte de l'Enfer, et la Statue de Balzac.* These statues were strategically placed in the garden. Behind the museum there is a beautiful pond from which there is an equally beautiful view of the dome of Les Invalides where Napoleon is buried.

Next was a visit to the Panthéon, considered Soufflot's masterpiece. It sits very near Luxembourg Gardens on the Rue Soufflot and houses the tombs of France's great. However, the first things of interest are the canvas paintings along the wall dedicated to the history of Sainte Geneviève, patron saint of Paris. Also in the center is Foucault's pendulum demonstrating the rotation of the earth. In the crypt are the tombs of Voltaire, Rousseau, Soufflot, Alexander Dumas, Pierre and Marie Curie just to name a few.

Next we wanted to see la Sainte-Chapelle, that beautiful miniature Gothic church built to house the relics of the Holy

Land, specifically the Crown of Thorns. The gold fleur-de-lys on the first level painted on an azure background catches your eye immediately, but the real beauty is in the upper level where the 15 stained glass windows are located. It's best to keep your fingers crossed for a sunny day when visiting so that the real beauty of the windows is revealed. These 15 windows tell the story of man from genesis through Christ's resurrection.

Since my friend was interested in painting, I felt that a visit to the Orangerie Museum was necessary. We had already visited Monet's Gardens, why not see the display of his Waterlilies, painted on 4 separate canvasses stitched together? There is a seating area in the center of the room where you can study these beautiful flowers.

That afternoon we also visited the Musée d'Orsay where you can see many many Impressionist paintings.

Not too far away from the Musée d'Orsay is the Rue du Bac. This time I wanted my friend to see the famous chapel, *Nôtre-Dame de la Médaille Miraculeuse*. It was here that the Virgin Mary appeared to Sister Catherine Labouré and requested that she create a medal which later became the miraculous medal. I had visited this site before so I had a vague idea of where I was going, but it is not on the beaten path of tourists. While I was there, I got some of the medals for my Catholic friends.

The next day was our last full day, and we had yet to see the beautiful blue stained glass windows of the Gothic Cathedral at Chartes. So we went to Gare Montparnasse to board the train to Chartres. When we arrived, there was a mass going on since it was Sunday morning. It was

222

interesting to see a mass in French. When the service was over, we got to photograph the cathedral. Then it was time to catch the return train. It was interesting to note that after we purchased our train tickets, no one on the train either coming or going ever asked us to show our tickets.

When we returned to Paris, we opted for a Bateaux-Mouches ride on the Seine. It was a beautiful sunny afternoon and a fitting way to end a trip—floating along the Seine on a riverboat and seeing the beautiful monuments in review. This was the best trip of my life because I got to show my beloved city to my beloved friend.

I did take one more trip with my friend. It was the following year, 2011, but it was not the same caliber as the one before. The tour company was the same: Grand European Tours. This time it was a trip to France, Switzerland, Italy Austria, and Germany. There was an extension to England that we opted to add at the beginning of the trip. So we got a flight from Cincinnati to Dulles, then another flight to Heathrow. In London we stayed at the Thistle Marble Arch Hotel which was at the end of Hyde Park. We were on our own in London to do as we wished. I wanted to see the famous department store, Harrods.

That store is spectacular. You can buy anything there, and you certainly can get lost there. I bought some refrigerator magnets, and in the processes lost my umbrella and the souvenir magnets because I fell in love with a white stuffed mechanical dog that walked and barked and came in his own cage. I wanted to buy that dog so badly, but there was no way that it would fit into my suitcase. Also this was the first day of a 19-day trip, and I did not want to carry it around Europe for the remainder of the tour. However I lost my concentration agonizing over that stuffed dog, and in the process put down my umbrella and magnets. Trying to retrace my steps was impossible, and we had other sites to see so we left Harrods without the umbrella and magnets.

Our next stop was the Tate Museum, then Westminster Abbey. Inside the abbey are buried many of the great writers and poets. Many are commemorated in and around Poets' Corner. We saw graves or memorial plaques of Chaucer, Robert Browning, Tennyson, and Kipling just to name a few. I found it interesting that most of Europe charges for each museum, but does not charge for entry to a church or cathedral. England, however, does the reverse. The museums are free, but there was a charge of 12 pounds each ($18.00) to visit Westminster Abbey. It was explained to me that if it were not for the fees, they would not be able to maintain Westminster because they have little or no attendance now.

Besides Westminster Abbey, there is another famous Church, St. Paul's Cathedral, built by Christopher Wren after the Great Fire of London. There is a saying, "Rob Peter to pay Paul". That saying comes from the fact that at one time the government helped support the Church of England, and the money destined for Westminster Abbey (the proper name is the Abbey of St. Peter's) was secretly switched to help repair St. Paul's Cathedral which also is in London.

There is one other interesting fact about England that separates them from Europe proper. Europe uses Euros for their money, but England still uses the Pound as their unit of currency. For dinner we had planned to eat at the Golden

Hind since it was written up as a great place to dine so we decided to find it. When we got to the restaurant, it was just a hole in the wall. The waiters were all sitting outside on the curb smoking, and the interior looked drab and unpleasant so we opted for a fish and chips restaurant near our hotel.

The next morning we had a group tour of Trafalgar Square. Afterwards my friend and I visited the Portrait Gallery and the National Gallery. Then we ate at Coventry Garden and toured the British Museum. On the way back to the hotel, I stopped again at Harrods and asked them if they had a Lost and Found Department in the store. The sales clerk in the cosmetic department told me yes, but it was hidden down in the basement and difficult to find so she lead me directly to where it was. There was an office and a man in charge so I told him that the day before, I had left a package at the store which contained my umbrella and 2 souvenir magnets. He had a large book that he looked through which had many pages. Also there was some kind of order to his book. He found the right page which had a number on it, and then he turned around and rummaged through many sacks in the rows of packages behind him and pulled out the package with my souvenirs. What a find! And what a system! That store has a great Lost and Found Department. I had waited just the right amount of time to claim my souvenirs. Had I gone there immediately, my souvenirs would not have had time to be put into the system.

The next morning my friend and I made our way to St. Pancras Station to catch the Eurostar Train to Paris. On the train we met six other tourists who were also part of our group. The train left at 9:00 A.M. and arrived at Gare du Nord at 12:47 P.M. Since there were eight of us all going to the same hotel, and I was the only one who could speak French, I told them I would try to find a cab that could take all of us. There were several large cabs across from the entrance to the station, and I found one willing to take all eight of us to our hotel, Pullman Paris Rive Gauche. So with our suitcases, we all squeezed into the cab, and I got to converse with the driver in French during our ride. The hotel was not centrally located but way across town at the end of the Ballad Subway Stop. The hotel was nice, but it was not a good location because nothing of interest was within walking distance.

After we settled in, we took the Metro to the Eiffel Tower, but there were long lines, and you needed to be part of a tour that had made previous arrangements in order to avoid the lines. Not wanting to spend the rest of the afternoon in a queue, we decided against this idea for the present time. We returned to the hotel for the group meeting. The next morning we could sign up for an optional tour of the Eiffel Tower so we did. It appears that the tour companies have a special arrangement with the Eiffel Tower Company so that their tourists do not have to stand in line. (Photo #50) The remainder of the day was spent in my favorite pastime, walking the streets of Paris.

Photo #50

The next morning our bus driver arrived so we traveled to Beaune for lunch then on to Lucerne for a two nights' stay. The morning tour included a visit to one of my favorite monuments, the Lion of Lucerne, commemorating the death of the Swiss Guards who lost their lives during the French Revolution defending King, Louis XVI. The lion is depicted with a broken spear in his shoulder, with his paw on the fleur-de-lys emblem, and with his face in the grips of death. Also the setting of this monument is beautiful and serene with the wounded lion casting his image on the pond below. Next we took an optional tour of Mt. Stanserhorn climbing to the top using a combination funicular and aerial cable car. The view of Lucerne from the top of the Mt. Stanserhorn is outstanding. Later we were treated to a lake cruise of Lake Lucerne.

The following day we were off through the Alps and the Italian Lake District to the Riviera. In the evening we drove along the Three Cornices to the same restaurant that we had visited the previous year, called Chez Cotton. The next day was a free day so we opted for a visit to the famous Océanographique Aquarium of Monaco where we were treated to all kinds of different beautiful fish. The Aquarium sits high on a hill on the coast, and we chose to walk all around the bay to our destination. The dinner that night was a famous restaurant in Monaco.

We were off to Pisa the next morning where we had time to walk around the Leaning Tower and visit the Cathedral of Pisa. Then we had to hurry along in order to get to Florence to see the famous statue of David which stands in the Academy of Fine Arts. There are other imitation statues of David inplace, but this is the original one. There were long lines everywhere and even though we had made prior arrangements, we still had to queue-up for this event. While standing in line, there were several vendors trying to tempt us with their original paintings.

The next morning we had time for a tour of Florence before leaving for Rome. Our next morning's tour of Rome included St. Peter's Basilica, the Sistine Chapel, a tour of the Spanish Steps, the Pantheon, and Trevi Fountain. However there was a large crowd at the fountain, and it was difficult to get a picture taken with the fountain in the background. It would have been just as difficult to get close enough to throw a coin over your shoulder into the fountain. For dinner we returned to Piazza Navona where we had dinner before. The restaurant is quite popular because it overlooks this piazza with the Fountains of the Four Rivers as a backdrop. Now so far the trip was going well. I had no idea of the approaching disaster. This time we had an evening floor show with audience participation. Wouldn't you know that one of the entertainers would choose my friend to go up on stage and simulate singing a famous Italian song. He did a super job imitating an Italian tenor while I videotaped him.

The next morning's plans included a full day tour of Pompeii. My friend being a history buff was looking forward to this trip; however that morning after breakfast when it was time to get on the bus, my friend told me through the bathroom door to go ahead and get on the bus, and tell Peter, our guide, that he would be right down. So I did that. In a few minutes my friend arrived and was deep in a conversation with Peter. Apparently there was a problem with bleeding hemorrhoids, and there was no way that he could sit on a bus in that condition. I was told that my friend wanted me to go on without him so I did. But the trip was long, and the walking was dangerous. I missed having the arm of my friend for support. Fortunately one of the women on our trip took pity on me, and offered her arm in support. Walking in Pompeii consists of manoeuvring from stone to stone, balancing as you walk. Also I had my video camera plus my friend's camera so I was walking and taking pictures at the same time—a very dangerous thing to do. So I appreciated all the help I could get.

That optional trip went on forever. It was long, and the walking was, in my opinion, dangerous. On our return we

229

stopped at a rest stop, and I bought my friend a sandwich. When we finally arrived at our hotel, I found that my friend had another disability to contend with. It seems that he had gone into Rome at my departure and got himself a sandwich to eat. However In the process of eating the sandwich, he broke off the bottom 2-3 teeth so now we have two problems to contend with: hemorrhoids and broken teeth.

The next day it was another attack of the hemorrhoids, and this time it was really serious. The bleeding would not stop so an ambulance was called. My friend was on his way to the hospital, and the trip went on without us. I was not allowed to ride in the ambulance so I had the hotel call me a cab, and I tried to find where they had taken my friend. Fortunately I did find the hospital, and I stayed in the waiting room looking at a large board on the wall indicating when each patient would be seen by a doctor. The receptionist spoke no English so I used my French to find out where my friend was. Finally they patched him up, and we went to a pharmacy and then back to the hotel. I found it interesting that the hospital needed no payment for their services.

We had taken out the travel Insurance offered by the company. I made several calls to the insurance company trying to find out when they might pick us up. Then I would call our guide and complain that no action was being taken so he would call the insurance company again. That went on for another 3 hours with zero results. My last attempt to get us home did get us a little reaction from our travel insurance company. I explained the situation to them again. They informed me that we would have to return to the hospital and get an oxygen test, a kind of insurance that my friend would be alright to fly home at 35,000 feet. As a last resort perhaps we could get the hotel to call us a doctor for the oxygen consumption test. I was not enamored with either of these choices so I called the airlines directly and told them that we needed to go home right away. Then they asked us when we would like to leave. I replied that we would like to leave as soon as possible. Then they gave us the departure flights from Frankfort that we could use since our tour ended in Frankfort. I replied that I didn't want to fly from Frankfort. I wanted to fly from Rome. Well, that wasn't possible. I could change our departure time, but not our departure city. Only the tour agency in the U.S. could make that change.

Finally I asked my friend if he thought he was able to travel again. He said, "Yes" so I called our guide, Peter, once more to ask if we could get back on the trip if we caught a train to Venice. He assured me that we could so I called a taxi, and the two of us went off to catch a train to Venice. It was rather a hair-raising ride to the station because I told the driver that we didn't have much time to catch our train. So he put the car in fast gear and, like a maniac, blew the horn and swore at every car to get out of our way so that we could catch our train.

Now catching a train is not the easiest thing to do. The Rome train station was very busy, and I knew that there was a train to Venice leaving soon, but how to get tickets for that trip was not easy. There was a very long line that I assumed was a line to purchase tickets. Also there was a Traveler's Aid Room, and I thought that they could help us get through the procedure of buying a ticket without the long line, but they were of no help whatsoever. They just pointed to the ticket line that I had already seen, but I felt that getting in line would facilitate missing our train. So we are standing in the middle of the train station looking very lost when a man suddenly appeared from nowhere. He asked where we wanted to go, then grabbed our luggage and was off to a ticket machine. He wanted to know our destination so we told him that we wanted to go to Venice. He told us how much it would cost so we gave him the money to put in the machine, and out came our train tickets.

Now that we had our tickets, he was looking for his reward, so we gave him a nice tip for his help. He carried our suitcases over to the train tracks where he handed them over to another entrepreneur who looked at our tickets and loaded our suitcases on to the train. Of course, he also wanted a tip. However, thanks to those two entrepreneurs, we got our train to Venice arriving just a little after our friends on the tour. The only thing we missed was a visit to Assisi. So now we were back on the tour again. The tour members were surprised to see us since they left us at Rome all the while thinking that we were on our way back to the U.S. I found it interesting that is was easier to get back on the tour than it was returning to the U.S. So much for taking out Travel Insurance.

The rest of the trip went well. There were no more episodes like the ones in Rome. From Venice we went on to Innsbruck, then Mainz, where we boarded a boat for our cruise along the Rhine. The cruise treated us to views of castles, vinyards and the Siren called Lorelei. We viewed Lorelei without the legendary shipwreck.

We flew home from Frankfurt. But every time I visit Germany I think about a humorous episode that occurred on a student trip there. I saw one of my adult ladies exiting from the men's restroom in Munich. She had a smile on her face, and she told me that I was certainly right about the toilets being very different in Europe. When I asked her why she chose that particular restroom, she told me that she had figured out that the Herrentoilette was for women because she knew the differrence between hissen and herren. I didn't want to spoil her revelation so how could I tell her that Herren was the German word for men even though it might look like our word for her?

Now that I am back in the U.S., I am sure that my traveling days are over. Never have I had a scare like the one on this trip. Getting sick in Europe becomes a big problem because the airlines don't want a sick passenger on board, and the sick passenger doesn't want to stay in a foreign country. So now the only travel that I plan to do is in my mind with my many photos and videos to watch that remind me of all the great places that I have been and will never see again.

P.S. As soon as I got home, I went onto Harrod's Website and found that little white walking/barking dog that I was so enamoured with in London, and I ordered it. It is a special souvenir, and it now has a special place in my bedroom.

List of 45 Trips Abroad

#	Year	Tour Company	Destination
#1	1958	Brownell	England, Holland, Belgium, Germany, Austria, Italy, France, Switzerland
#2	1962	AAA	Spain, Portugal, France
#3	1963	Temple University Foreign language	France, Sorbonne
#4	1964	Study Abroad	Rome, Egypt, Lebanon, Syria, Jordon, Israel, Turkey, Greece
#5	1965	Study Abroad	Norway, Sweden, Denmark, Finland, Russia, Austria, Berlin
#6	1966	Foreign Language Study Tour	University of Reims, France, Switzerland
#7	1967	Travcoa Air	Around the World in 70 Days
#8	1968	Travcoa Air	African Safari in 69 Days
#9	1969	Travel-a-G0-Go	Guatamala
#10	1969-70	Compass Travel	Russian Winter
#11	1971	Russian language Study Tour	University of Leningrad England, Belgrade, Prague
#12	1972	Cook	Christmas in U.S.S.R.
#13	1973	FACETS	Student Trip to Paris
#14	1975	Cook	Student Trip to Finland and Russia
#15	1976	ALSG	Spring Trip to Madrid, Segovia, Avila, Toledo

#16	1978	ALSG	Student Trip to Paris & the Alps
#17	1981	Cultural Heritage	Student Trip to France & Switzerland
#18	1982	CHA	Student Trip to Austria, Switzerland & Germany
#19	1982	TWA	Driving Trip Thru Germany
#20	1983	CHA	Student Trip to German peaking Countries
#21	1986	CHA	Student Trip--Treasures of Europe
#22	1987	CHA	Student Trip to France & Switzerland
#23	1988	EF	Student Trip to France, Germany, & the Alps
#24	1989	EF	Student Trip to England & France
#25	1990	EF	Student Trip Vienna to the Rhine
#26	1991	EF	Student Trip to Paris & the Pyrenees
#27	1991	Insight	Summer Trip to Scandanavia & the Fjords
#28	1992	EF	Student Trip to Paris, Riviera, & the Alps
#29	1993	EF	Student Trip to Paris & the Châteaux
#30	1993	Globus	Spring Trip London & Ireland

Bicycle Trips

	Year	Company	Month	Destination
#31	1993	Elderhostel	Sept.	North Holland
#32	1994	Elderhostel	Sept.	Loire Valley, France.
#33	1995	Elderhostel	April	Danube, Austria, Vienna
#34	1995	Elderhostel	August	Denmark
#35	1996	Elderhostel	Sept.	East Anglia, England
#36	1997	Elderhostel	May	Bordeaux, France, Basque Coast
#37	1998	Elderhostel	Sept.	Salzach & Inn Rivers, Austria
#38	1999	Elderhostel	Sept.	South Holland
#39	2000	Elderhostel	Sept.	Italy, Austria
#40	2001	Elderhostel	May	Cotswolds & Chalk Downs, England
#41	2002	Elderhostel	May	Provence France
#42	2006	Elderhostel	Sept.	Barge Trip Rhine & Mosel Rivers, Germany
#43	2008	Elderhostel	May	Barge Trip Paris & Chateaux of Central France

Trips With My Friend

#44	2010	Grand European	Sept.	France
#45	2011	Grand European	Sept.	England, Paris, Lucerne, Monaco, Italy, Austria Germany

Photos

1. Carole in Beauty Contest aboard the M.S. Italia
2. Brussels and the Atomium, Belgium
3. Canal & the Bridge of Sighs, Venice
4. Carole & two of the San Marino Guards
5. Entrance to the Blue Grotto, Italy
6. Bay of Naples, Italy
7. Carole at the well in Fatima, Portugal
8. The Alhambra, Granada, Spain
9. Carcassonne, France
10. Amalfi Drive, Italy
11. Carole on Camel, Memphis, Egypt
12. Carole in front of the Sphinx in Giza, Egypt
13. Dead Sea Scrolls, West Bank
14. Garden of Gethsemane, Jerusalem
15. Terrace of Lions, Delos, Greek Isle near Mykonos
16. Island of Mykonos, Aegean Sea
17. Millesgarden, Stockholm, Sweden
18. East Berlin Cemetery, near the Wall
19. Manneken Pis, Brussels
20. Battle of Waterloo, Belgium
21. Pissoir, Reims, France
22. Horse Meat Shop, Reims, France
23. Tomb of Ste. Bernadette, Nevers, France
24. Carole at Deer Park, Nara, Japan
25. Ivory Catalog, Hong Kong
26. Banyon Temple, Angkor Thom, Cambodia
27. Galle Face Hotel, Colombo, Ceylon

28. Taj Mahal. Agra, India
29. Houseboat—The Triumph, The Vale of Kashmir, Srinagar
30. Carole & King of Swat, near Khyber Pass
31. Lunch delivered in Kabul, Afghanistan
32. Carboard toilet Seat, Timbuktu, Mali
33. The Big Hole, Kimberley, South Africa
34. Carole & Zulu Chief, Drummond, South Africa
35. Victoria Falls, Rhodesia
36. Masai Warriors, Lake Manyara, Tanganyika
37. Carole & Land Rover, Ngorongoro Crater, Tanganyika
38. Treetops, Kikkuyu Reserve, Kenya
39. Observation at Treetops, Kikkuyu Reserve, Kenya
40. Warning Sign, near Ft. Portal, Uganda
41. Pygmies at Mountains of Moon, Uganda
42. Father Frost, Nevsky Prospect, Leningrad
43. Kremlin Cathedrals around Red Square, Moscow
44. Troike Ride, Sokolniki Park, Moscow
45. Carole In Prison, Cremona Tower, Italy
46. Out of Prison, Cremona, Italy
47. Carole as Sweep of the Day, Elderhostel Bicycle Trip
48. Carole & Statue, both down in the dumps, Paris
49. My friend and I at Pont du Gard, Nimes
50. My friend and I near Eiffel Tower, Champ de Mars, Paris

Notes About the Cover

When I started traveling in 1958, the hotels used to give you luggage stickers for your suitcase. It was common to ask for them when checking out. I have several hundred luggage stickers from Europe, Africa, and Around the World. So you will find an assortment of them on the front and back covers. I don't know when the hotels stopped distributing them, but if you asked for any today, I fear you would get a blank stare.

CPSIA information can be obtained at www.ICGtesting.com
Printed in the USA
LVOW05*0902080913

351392LV00002B/5/P